THE

Inner

Treasure

Also by Jonathan Star

Rumi:
In the Arms
of the Beloved

A Garden
Beyond Paradise
(WITH SHAHRAM SHIVA)

A Translation of
the *Tao Te Ching*

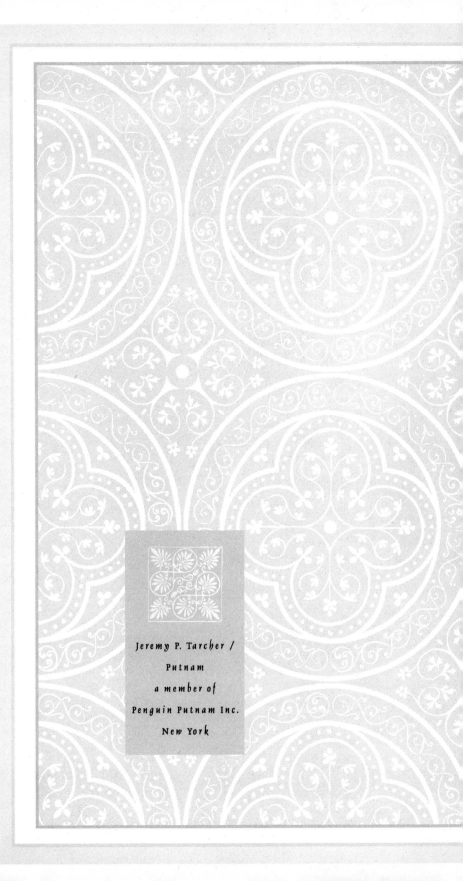

Jeremy P. Tarcher /
Putnam
a member of
Penguin Putnam Inc.
New York

T H E
Inner
Treasure

AN INTRODUCTION
TO THE WORLD'S
SACRED AND
MYSTICAL WRITINGS

Jonathan Star

Most Tarcher/Putnam books are available at special quantity
discounts for bulk purchase for sales promotions, premiums,
fund-raising, and educational needs. Special books or book excerpts
also can be created to fit specific needs. For details, write Putnam
Special Markets, 375 Hudson Street, New York, NY 10014.

Jeremy P. Tarcher/Putnam
a member of
Penguin Putnam Inc.
375 Hudson Street
New York, NY 10014
www.penguinputnam.com

Jonathan Star can be contacted at: unity10@aol.com

Library of Congress Cataloging-in-Publication Data

Star, Jonathan.
    The inner treasure: an introduction to the world's
sacred and mystical writings / Jonathan Star.
        p.   cm.
    Includes bibliographical references.
    ISBN 0-87477-971-5 (alk. paper)
    1. Sacred books.   I. Title.
BL70.S735   1999   98-54702 CIP
291.8'2—dc21

Printed in the United States of America
10 9 8 7 6 5 4 3 2 1

This book is printed on acid-free paper. ∞

BOOK DESIGN BY DEBORAH KERNER

Contents

Preface

A FUNDAMENTAL TEACHING OF THE WORLD'S RELIG-
ious and mystical traditions is that the source of love, the fulfillment of life, and the treasure of heaven are found within. This is
the discovery made by all those who have realized the highest
truth of each tradition. We hear this message reflected in Jesus'
words: "The kingdom of heaven is within"; in the poems of Kabir:
"Listen, the Lord of all plays his song within you"; and in the teachings of great masters who say: "God dwells in the human heart," or
"The God you seek is your own self."

Each tradition is made whole by those who have followed the
path to the end, and who have come to know that the God they
sought was their own soul. Each tradition remains alive through the
wisdom and experience of these great beings who live in the pure
spirit of God and who grant the divine grace that allows a human
being to experience his oneness with the Absolute. The Sufi Master
Ibn al Arabi writes, "When the mysterious unity between the soul
and the Divine becomes clear, you will realize that you are none
other than God. You will see all your actions as His actions; all your
features as His features; all your breaths as His breath."

Although these enlightened souls have the same essential experience—of being one with the Absolute—they are described by
various names. The Taoists call them *Sheng Jen,* "those who hear
the voice of the Absolute"; the yogis call them *Siddhas,* "perfect beings"; the Buddhists call them *Buddhas,* "the awakened ones." To
the Sufis they are *Shaykh, Murshid,* or *Pir,* "Master"; to the Christians they are *Saints.* An Indian sage, Ramdasa, writes: "That which
is impossible to attain by men becomes possible only through con-
tact with Saints. Saints indeed are truly rich, for they possess in
their hands the keys of the spiritual treasure . . . There is no limit
to the greatness of the Saints, for it is on account of them that God
is revealed."

The poems and stories in this collection offer us a glimpse of the vision and experience of these great beings. Each word uttered by an enlightened soul is infused with divinity and the power of direct experience; and their words have the ability to bring us into their world, put us into their company, and coax us inward so that we may experience our own greatness. Their words guide us to a magical place within—a world of pulsating consciousness, supreme peace, unbounded love, infinite beauty; a world where all the universe is united in a grand fellowship of bliss. So come, enter this wonder, and let these divine words reveal to us the truth that is forever our own.

—JONATHAN STAR

T H E

Inner
Treasure

The Scriptures of India

INDIA'S VAST RELIGIOUS HERITAGE IS ROOTED IN THE ancient and sublime scriptures of Sanskrit. The oldest scriptures of India, the *Vedas* (literally "knowledge," or "sacred teachings"), are a vast collection of Sanskrit hymns, prayers, and rituals, composed between the fifteenth and tenth centuries B.C. These works are divided into four books: the **Rig Veda,** the Veda of hymns, which praises the gods, the elements, and the bounty of earth; the *Yajur Veda*, the Veda of sacrificial texts; the *Sama Veda*, the Veda of songs; and the *Atharva Veda*, the Veda of Atharva, overseer of the sacred fire ceremony. The *Rig Veda* is the first Veda—and the oldest existing scripture of India.

At the end of each Veda is a section called the **Upanishads,** which literally means, "sitting close, with devotion." This final section of each Veda contains the "secret teachings" of the ancients, which, over the centuries, have been well-guarded and meant for the most worthy disciples. The *Upanishads* inquire into the nature of reality, God, and the universe. They are more probing than the rest of the Vedas, and they address the essential issue of how a seeker can attain God-Realization. The *Upanishads* teach that the Absolute Reality, *Brahman*, dwells fully in the human soul; and that this Reality is meant to be known. The teachings of the *Upanishads* are called *Vedanta*, which means "at the end of the Vedas."

Another treasure of Indian spirituality, originating between the fifth and second centuries B.C., is the *Mahabharata*, a sweeping epic that follows the struggle between the two sides of the Bharata family. This extensive work is filled with popular myth, legends, and spiritual lessons, but at its core, it is about the path of *dharma* (righteousness, truth, duty). Within this grand poetic drama lies the **Bhagavad Gita** (*The Song of God*), which is among the most famous and revered dialogues in all religious literature. The *Bha-*

gavad Gita opens when the final battle between the two sides of the Bharata family (the righteous side versus the unrighteous side) is about to begin. The famed archer Arjuna and his charioteer, Lord Krishna, ride out between the two opposing armies. When Arjuna sees his teachers and cousins on one side and his brothers on the other, he becomes utterly dejected and full of doubt about his duty (*dharma*) as a warrior: "Letting fall his bow and arrows, Arjuna slumps into his chariot, dejected, his spirit stunned by grief." Seeing Arjuna's condition, Krishna begins to instruct Arjuna about *dharma* and truth, about knowledge, right action, and the path of union with God (*yoga*). But his words are not enough to rouse Arjuna into action. Krishna then reveals his true identity as the Lord of the universe and shows Arjuna a vision of his all-pervasive form. By this transcendent understanding of the universe, and his role in it, Arjuna regains his vigor and is ready to fight. On a nearby hill sits the sage Sanjaya, who narrates the whole story to the blind king, Dhritarashtra.

Within the *Mahabharata* is another well-known section called the **Vishnu Sahasranam** (*The Thousand Names of Vishnu*), a compendium of a thousand different aspects, powers, and forms of the Supreme Lord. (In the Hindu Trinity, which describes the three aspects of God, Brahma is the Creator, Vishnu is the Sustainer, and Shiva is the Destroyer.) This Sanskrit scripture is often chanted aloud in order to invoke the many sustaining powers of God. According to Swami Muktananda, "The Supreme Being is the most radiant of all lights, and so are His Thousand Names. The highest austerity lies in reciting the *Vishnu Sahasranam*. I have practiced it for years, and as a result I have reaped the full reward. It is through the practice of this chant that I have been able to experience the divine light and power. This very chant is the supreme God manifest as sound . . . The reward of singing this chant is the fulfillment of any desire which may arise in the heart."

The **Avadhuta Gita** (date unknown) is a Sanskrit text describing the position of Non-dual (*Advaita*) Vedanta. It is a work that reads like a repetitive chant, again and again proclaiming the outlook of absolute unity. This text is written from the perspective of an *Avadhuta*. An *Avadhuta* is a liberated soul who is completely beyond worldly attachments and cares. He seeks nothing, he renounces nothing; he is not swayed by social convention nor approval. He exists completely in the bliss of his own inner self. This work is customarily attributed to the sage Dattatreya.

Rig Veda ⁂
HYMN OF CREATION

In the beginning
There was neither existence nor nonexistence,
Neither sky nor heaven beyond . . .

That One breathed, without breath,
By His own breathless power.

The first born was the Creative Will,
The primordial seed of the mind.
All else followed.
The sages, searching for the truth within themselves,
Discovered the eternal bond between the seen and unseen.
This bond was an endless line stretched across the heavens.
What was above?
What was below?
Primal seeds were sprouting, mighty forces were moving;
Pulsation from below, pure energy above.

Who here knows? Who can say for sure? . . .
When it began and from where it came—this creation?
The gods came afterwards—
So who really knows?

From where this creation came,
By what means it was formed,
Only He who watches from the highest heaven knows—
    or perhaps even He does not know!

Shvetashvatara Upanishad ≫
THE INFINITE ONE

Though the Infinite One is without color,
He colors the entire universe;
Though immortal,
He is born, and lives, and dies.
That One is all that was, and is, and will be,
Yet He is always the same.

He is the Supreme, Unchanging, Absolute.

He becomes the fire, the sun,
The wind, and the moon.
He becomes the starry heavens,
And the vast waters, giving life to all.

He becomes the woman, the man,
The youth, and the maiden too.
He becomes the old fellow
Tottering on his staff.
He becomes every face
Looking in every direction.

He becomes the blue butterfly,
The green parrot with red eyes.
He becomes lightning, the seasons,
The endless seas.

Without birth or death,
Beyond all time and space,
He is the One from whom
All the worlds are born.

Mandukya Upanishad ⠶

THE LORD OF ALL

Dwelling in every heart,
    the Self is the Lord of all,
    the seer of all,
    the source and goal of all.
The Self is not outer awareness,
It is not inner awareness,
Nor is it the suspension of awareness.
It is not knowing,
It is not unknowing,
Nor is it knowingness itself.
It cannot be seen nor grasped,
It cannot be contained.
It is beyond all expression
    and beyond all thought.
It is indefinable.

The only way to know it is to become it.

It is the final resting place of all activity,
    silent and unchanging,
    the Supreme Good,
    One without a second.
It is the Supreme Self.
It, above all else, should be known.

Bhagavad Gita ❧
DIVINE MANIFESTATIONS

Lord Krishna:

I am the source of everything,
and all worlds come out of Me;
Knowing this, the wise ones honor me
in the cave of their hearts.

To those with unswerving devotion,
who worship me with love,
I give the boon of discrimination
by which they come to me.

Dwelling within
as pure consciousness,
I destroy the darkness born of ignorance
with the shining lamp of truth.

I am the Supreme Self
dwelling in the hearts of all creatures.
They are born in me, sustained by me,
and in the end, return to me.

Listen, Arjuna, my divine power
is endless in extent,
And so I can only tell you of
my most prominent forms:

Of sun gods I am Vishnu,
of lights, the radiant sun;
I am chief among the wind gods,
the moon in the starry sky.

Among rituals, I am the chanting of sacred names,
among gods, I am Indra, lord of heaven;
Among sense-organs, I am the mind,
and the pure intellect of all beings.

I am the glorious Shiva among gods of destruction,
the Lord of Wealth among keepers of fortune;
I am the pure flame among the fire gods,
the great Meru among mountain peaks.

O Arjuna, I am the guru of the gods,
and chief of heavenly priests;
Of generals I am Skanda, god of war,
of bodies of water, I am the ocean.

Among great sages, I am Brighu,
among words, I am the eternal sound *Om*;
Of sacrifices, I am the repetition of God's Name,
of all that is immovable, I am the Himalayas.

Among trees, I am the holy fig tree,
and Narada among divine seers;
I am the leader of heavenly musicians,
the sage Kapila among perfected souls.

Of horses, I am the radiant stallion,
born from the ocean of pure nectar;
Among royal elephants, I am the king's mount;
among men, their loyal protector.

I am the thunderbolt among weapons,
the wish-fulfilling cow among cattle;
I am the god of love begetting children,
and Vasuki, king of the snakes.

I am the endless serpent, Ananta,
the lord of all sea creatures;
I am Aryaman, the greatest ancestor,
and the Lord of Death, who reckons every deed.

I am Prahlada, the devoted son of demons,
and Time, the measure of all that endures;
I am the lion among beasts,
and the Lord's eagle among birds.

Of purifiers, I am the wind,
and the great Rama among warriors;
I am the shark among sea creatures,
and the River Ganges among all waters that flow.

O Arjuna! Of all creation
I am the beginning, middle, and end;
I am the supreme knowledge of the Self,
the eloquence of every orator.

Of letters, I am the letter *A*,
of compounds, the simple pairing;
I am the Creator facing all directions
and time inexhaustible.

I am Death, devourer of all,
and also the origin of all things yet to be;
Among feminine virtues I am fame, fortune,
eloquence, gratitude, patience, and forgiveness . . .

I am the Great Chant of the ancients,
the meter of Vedic hymns;
I am the first cool month of the year,
the Spring bursting with flowers.

I am the loaded dice of tricksters,
the radiance of shining heroes;
I am victory, effort,
and the wisdom among the wise.

I am Krishna among the mighty Vrishnis,
and Arjuna among the Pandava princes;
I am the great Vyasa among sages,
and Ushanas the illumined poet.

I am the judging rod of rulers,
the shrewd tactics of ambitious men;
I am the silence of secret things,
the truth of ancient knowledge.

O Arjuna, I am the primal seed
of all existence;
No being, moving or unmoving,
can exist without me.

O Great Warrior, there is no end
to the forms of my divine power . . .

All that exists,
all that is beautiful, radiant, and powerful,
is but a spark
of my brilliant Light . . .

And here I stand, supporting the entire world,
with one fragment of my being.

Bhagavad Gita ⟫

Lord Krishna:

Arjuna, behold my forms
in the hundreds and the thousands;
They are varied, divine,
of every shape and hue.

See the celestial deities, gods of fire,
gods of destruction, twin gods of dawn,
and also gods of thunder.
Arjuna, behold these wonders never seen before.

See the whole of this universe,
the movable and immovable,
and whatever else you wish to see,
unified, as one, in my body.

Your own eyes
cannot truly see me,
So I will give you divine sight
to behold the glory of my wondrous form!

Sanjaya (narrating to the King from a nearby hill):

Having thus spoken, O King,
The Great Lord of Yoga
revealed to Arjuna
his supreme form.

It was a wondrous vision of the infinite Lord,
with faces and eyes everywhere;
With celestial ornaments
and heavenly weapons of every kind.

The stream of sights was endless,
displaying every possible marvel;
Divine garments and garlands,
the heavens filled with ambrosial perfume.

If the light of a thousand suns
were to blaze together in the sky,
such would hardly match the splendor
of that Great Being.

Arjuna:

I see your infinite form—
arms, bellies, faces, and eyes everywhere.
I see no beginning, middle, or end.
O Lord of the Universe, you are everything!

I see your crown, club, and discus,
your radiant light on all sides;
It is hard to look at this blaze of fire and sun
that fills your immeasurable form.

You are the supreme goal of all knowledge,
the ultimate refuge of all the world;
You are the guardian of eternal law,
the innermost spirit of all.

I see your endless power becoming everything.
I see the sun and moon in your eyes,
the all-consuming fire of your mouth,
the radiance of your light filling the skies.

O Great One, you alone fill
the space between heaven and earth.
Seeing your wondrous and awesome form,
all the worlds cower in fear.

I see the hosts of gods entering you,
others, in fear, bow their heads and ask for mercy.
Throngs of great seers and perfected beings
praise you with the glorious chanting of your Name.

Gods of destruction, gods of light,
celestial beings, angels, heavenly horsemen,
howling wind gods, ancestors,
throngs of heavenly musicians, magical beings,
demons, and those with supernatural powers,
all look at you in wonder.

Seeing your great form,
your countless mouths and eyes,
your numerous arms, legs, feet, bellies,
and terrible fangs, O Krishna
all the worlds tremble,
and so do I.

O Supreme Lord
tell me who you are in so frightful a form?

Lord Krishna:

I am the all-powerful Time, destroyer of every world,
relentlessly moving all things to their end.
even without you, these warriors
arrayed in opposing armies will not survive.

So stand up and win glory!
Conquer your enemies
and enjoy the fullness of your rightful kingdom.
They have already been slain by me.
O peerless archer,
be the instrument of my will.

Arjuna:

You are the First Being,
the ancient soul of man,
the ultimate resting place of all worlds.
You are the knower, the known,
and the state beyond knowing.
All the universe is filled by you,
O Lord of Infinite Forms.

I thought you were my peer
and rashly called you
"Krishna," "son of Yadu," "friend";
through negligence, or the blindness of my love,
I could not see your greatness.

You are Father of the world,
the object of its worship,
the most venerable of its masters.
You are without equal.
Who in the three worlds could ever
surpass your incomparable might?

Lord Krishna:

This vision you have seen
is indeed rare;
even the gods are ever-wishing
for such a sight.

Not through study of the scriptures,
austerities, charity, or sacrifice
can I be seen as you have seen me.

O Arjuna, only by the
unswerving love of the heart
can my supreme state be seen,
and known, and attained.

Bhagavad Gita
I SHALL DO YOUR BIDDING

Lord Krishna:

Relying on your own senses,
harboring false compassion,
you think, "I will not fight";
but your resolve is in vain,
your own nature will compel you.

You were born in this world with a duty,
decreed by your own destiny.
O Arjuna, what delusion now turns you
against your own calling?

The Supreme Lord dwells in the heart of all beings,
and by His magic power of illusion
He causes them to move about like wooden dolls
on a spinning wheel.

Give your whole heart to that Supreme Lord,
seek refuge in Him alone;
By His Grace you will find perfect peace
and the abode of immortal life.

Go deeper and deeper within yourself
until nothing is left—then fight!
No one on earth is more dear to me than you.
That is why I tell you all this . . .

Abandon all hope of gain from this world
and take refuge in me alone;
I will wash away your sins
and free you from every evil.
You will never grieve again.

Fix your mind on me,
think of yourself as me;
worship me, sacrifice to me,
honor me as your own Self,
and you will surely come to me.
This I promise you,
for you are dear to me . . .

Arjuna! Have you heard me?
Have my words hit their mark?

Arjuna:

O Krishna,
Through your grace
the foe of delusion has been destroyed;
the clear light of wisdom has dawned.
Now I am determined,
with every doubt dispelled—
O Lord,
I stand here, ready, to do as you command.

Avadhuta Gita ❧

I am neither created nor uncreated, for I have always been here.
I am neither deluded nor undeluded, for I have always been here.
I am neither of light nor of darkness, for I have always been here.
> I am the Bliss, I am the Truth, I am the Boundless Sky.

How can I speak of having desires or not having desires?
How can I speak about attachment or non-attachment?
How can I speak about God as being real or unreal?
> I am the Bliss, I am the Truth, I am the Boundless Sky.

That One is everything— How can I say it is one?
How can I say it is more than one?
How can I say it is eternal or noneternal?
> I am the Bliss, I am the Truth, I am the Boundless Sky.

It is neither solid nor subtle; neither appearing nor disappearing.
It is without beginning, middle, or end.
It is neither above nor below.
This is the secret of the Ultimate Truth.
> I am the Bliss, I am the Truth, I am the Boundless Sky.

All your senses are like clouds;
All they show is an endless mirage.
The Radiant One is neither bound nor free.
> I am the Bliss, I am the Truth, I am the Boundless Sky.

Dear one, I am not unknowable nor hidden.
I am not imperceivable nor lost.
I am not near nor far.
> I am the Bliss, I am the Truth, I am the Boundless Sky.

I am the fire that burns away the karma of one beyond karma.
I am the fire that burns away the sorrow of one beyond sorrow.
I am the fire that burns the body of one without a body.
> I am the Bliss, I am the Truth, I am the Boundless Sky.

I destroy the sins of one who is sinless.
I destroy the attributes of one without attributes.
I destroy the bonds of one without bounds.
    I am the Bliss, I am the Truth, I am the Boundless Sky.

Dear one, I neither exist nor do I not exist.
I am not one nor am I many.
I am neither conscious nor do I lack consciousness.
    I am the Bliss, I am the Truth, I am the Boundless Sky.

I do not will that the Truthful One seems deluded.
I do not will that the Blissful One seems in despair.
I do not will that the All-Giving One seems to be taking.
    I am the Bliss, I am the Truth, I am the Boundless Sky.

The vines of earthliness do not entangle me.
The promise of peace does not allure me.
The bondage of ignorance does not touch me.
    I am the Bliss, I am the Truth, I am the Boundless Sky.

The world of activity is not part of me.
The pain of laziness is not part of me.
The purity of one's own duty is not part of me.
    I am the Bliss, I am the Truth, I am the Boundless Sky.

I have no actions that bring regret or misery.
I have no thoughts that bring pain or suffering.
I have no sense of "me" or "mine."
    I am the Bliss, I am the Truth, I am the Boundless Sky.

Vishnu Sahasranam ※
THE THOUSAND NAMES OF GOD

Om,
The form of that One is the entire universe:

That One is called *Vishnu,*
 The Supreme Being who
 enters everything and everyone.
Lord of all time,
Creator of all life,
Sustainer of all worlds,
He becomes everything in the universe
 without losing His pure existence.
He evolves and nourishes all creatures.
Indeed, He is the Supreme Self of all.

That One is called *Shiva,*
 The Radiant One.
Ever-free, without death or decay,
 He is the highest goal of liberated ones.
Witnessing everything
 without aid or instrument,
Steady, immovable, and changeless,
He is the source of all existence,
 the one attainable through yoga.

That One is called *Ishvara,*
 The one with unlimited power over all things.
He is the changeless and indestructible Being,
 the one in whom the whole universe merges,
 and remains,
 at the time of cosmic dissolution.

That One is called *Shambhu,*
 The bestower of supreme bliss.

Born of His own free will,
  supporting the universe and its substratum,
  He exists of Himself, uncaused by another.

That One is called *Uttama,*
  The greatest of all beings.
Having one existence,
  without birth or death,
He is the Eternal, the most ancient,
The ultimate support of all things.
He is the One who cannot be grasped
  by the senses
    nor conceived by the mind.

That One is called *Manu,*
  The one whose thoughts become the universe.
His sight gives purity to everything,
  His breath gives life to everything,
  His lips give joy to everything.
He is the Supremely Auspicious One
  whose remembrance removes all obstacles.

That One is called *Prana,*
  The Supreme force that
  controls and regulates everything.
He gives the power of breath to every creature.
Master of all living beings,
Container of all creation,
He can be known through
  silence, meditation, and the practice of yoga.

That One is called *Kirti,*
  The root of all action,
  the sum total of all human achievement.
Eternal,
Requiring no other support,

He is the seed of the universe,
    the one to whom all beings owe their existence.
"Where is He established, O Lord?"—
    In His own greatness.

That One is called *Sharma*,
    The Supreme Bliss.
Granting every object of desire,
    dwelling in all beings,
He is the one whose form
    cannot be measured by time or space.
He stands completely aside from all limitations.
Lord of all Lords, supremely tranquil,
There is no doubt—He is the Luminous One.

That One is called *Satya*,
    The Eternal Truth.
Equally present in all beings,
Unlimited by any entity,
Standing free of all bondage,
He is the one whose every resolution comes true,
    whose worship always bears fruit.
O seeker,
    Look and you will find Him in the lotus of your heart.

That One is called *Rudra*,
    The remover of sorrow.
Knowing everything and shining everywhere,
Bestowing perfect knowledge of the universe,
Destroying all ignorance,
He is free from every defect.
He is the greatest of all good fortune,
The Supreme Destination,
    The attainment from which there is no return.

That One is called *Kavi*,
    The witness to the play of this world.
Purifying all those who adore Him,
Possessing infinite power,
Ruler of everything within and without,
He is the one whose actions never go to waste.
He dwells again and again
    as the incarnated soul;
He is the one who must be known
    by those who seek realization.

That One is called *Madhu*,
    The sweetness of love and bliss.
One whose illumination is brighter than all lights,
Whose strength is greater than all powers,
Whose wisdom surpasses all knowing.
Self-illumined,
The Spirit beyond all measure,
Endowed with greatness of every kind,
He bestows the highest destiny
    to those whose hearts are pure.

That One is called *Maharishi*,
    The supreme virtue of realized beings.
The power of all worlds,
The remover of all fears,
The doer of all things;
He is the supreme brilliance,
The ultimate support,
The Father of all who are born.

The Sages of Taoism

BETWEEN THE SIXTH AND THIRD CENTURIES B.C., THE dominant philosophy in China was Confucianism. This humanistic philosophy emphasized filial piety, responsibilities, and man's obligation to the social order. Although Confucianism offered a re-assuring structure for civilized life—a structure that still remains in Chinese society—it did not address the yearnings of those who sought a more spiritual view of life. Taoism arose to fill this void, to put man back in touch with his spirit, his nature, and the forces that comprise the universe. Instead of emphasizing man's relation-ship to family and social order, Taoism called on seekers to find that higher power within; instead of emphasizing structure and rit-uals, the Taoist sages taught the virtues of simple living and flow-ing with nature. Moral excellence, proper conduct, and kindness toward others were not things that needed to be studied and learned; rather they were qualities that would unfold naturally when one came to know his own virtue and the goodness that was natural to his own soul.

Among the religious philosophies of the world, Taoism holds the distinction of being "soft": the All-Powerful Reality is praised for its weakness not its strength, for resembling a yielding female not a dominant male. *Tao* is not a fixed principle but the endless unfolding of the universe itself. The Supreme Principle, *Tao,* is fluid and alive and inseparable from one's own life. At its root, Taoism teaches that the splendor of this world, and the greatness of one's own being, are revealed through the natural flow of life.

The concept of *Tao* was first put forth in the **Tao Te Ching,** a short classic *(ching)* of five thousand words, which now stands as the central text of Taoism. The *Tao Te Ching* is a collection of say-ings gathered from the writings of Chinese sages between the sixth and second centuries B.C., and traditionally attributed to Lao Tzu. Blending together descriptions of nature, the actions of sages, mystical visions, spiritual counseling, and political advice, the *Tao Te Ching* tells of *Tao*, the Absolute Reality, and *Te*—how that Reality manifests. The simple yet profound teachings contained in this book have influenced every part of Chinese society—its philosophy, religion, art, medicine, and even its cooking. The Chinese translator Lionel Giles said of the *Tao Te Ching*: "The wording of the original is extraordinarily vigorous and terse; never, surely, has so much thought been compressed into so small a space. Throughout the universe there are scattered a certain number of stars belonging to a class known as 'white dwarfs.' They are usually very small, yet the atoms of which they consist are crushed together so closely that their weight is enormous in relation to their size, and this entails the radiation of so much energy that the surface is kept at a temperature vastly hotter than that of the sun. The *Tao Te Ching* may fitly be called a 'white dwarf' of philosophical literature, so weighty is it, so compact, and so suggestive of a mind radiating thought at a white heat."

The other work that forms the backbone of Taoism is the **Chuang Tzu,** a fanciful collection of stories written by Chuang Tzu in the fourth century B.C. This bold and satirical piece of writing pokes fun at philosophers, parochial scholars, and every school of thought that threatens to hold back the boundless spirit of man. While the *Tao Te Ching* celebrates the virtue of humility, Chuang Tzu tells of freedom, of wandering the earth, of soaring through the inner skies. In one of his famous lines he writes: "I did not know whether I was Chuang Tzu dreaming I was a butterfly, or a butterfly dreaming I was Chuang Tzu." The Chinese scholar Lin Yutang writes: "On the whole, Chuang-tsu must be considered the greatest prose writer of the Chou Dynasty. His claim to this position rests both upon the brilliance of his style and the depth of his thought. That explains the fact that although he was probably the greatest antagonist of Confucian ideas, no Confucian scholar has not openly or secretly admired him."

The **Lieh Tzu** is a minor collection of Taoist stories and parables supposedly written in the third century B.C.

Tao Te Ching ⫸
VERSE 1

That which can be called the Tao
    is not the Eternal Tao
That which can be called the Name
    is not the Eternal Name

Tao is both One and many
As One, it is the Nameless root
    of Heaven and Earth
As many, it is the apparent mother
    of all things

A mind free of its own desire
    beholds the true miracle of Tao
A mind lost in its own desire
    sees only the forms of this world

Tao and this world seem different
    but in truth they are one and the same
The only difference is in the name we give them

How deep and mysterious this Unity is
    How profound, how great!
It is the truth beyond the truth,
    the mystery beyond the mind
It is the path to all wonder,
    the gate to the ecstatic nature of everything!

Tao Te Ching ⁂

Something formless, complete in Itself
There before Heaven and Earth
Tranquil, vast, standing alone, unchanging
It provides for all things without being exhausted
It is the Mother of the Universe
I do not know its name
    so I call it "Tao"
Forced to name it further
I call it
    "Greater than the Greatest"
    "The End of all Endings"
I call it
    "That which is Beyond the Beyond"
    "That to which All Things Return"

From Tao comes all greatness—
    Greatness to Heaven
    Greatness to Earth
    Greatness to Man
Within the bounds of this world
    there are four great things
And Man is one of them

Man relies on the laws of Earth
Earth relies on the laws of Heaven
Heaven relies on the laws of Tao
But Tao relies on nothing but Itself
    Supremely free, Self-so, It is of its own nature

Tao Te Ching ⟫

Eyes look but cannot see It
Ears listen but cannot hear It
Hands grasp but cannot touch It
Beyond the senses lies this Unity—
     Invisible, Inaudible, Intangible

What rises up appears bright
What settles down appears dark
Yet in truth there is neither darkness nor light
     just an unbroken dance of shadows
From nothingness to fullness
     and back again to nothingness
This formless form,
This imageless image,
     cannot be grasped by mind or might
Try to face It—
     In what place will you stand?
Try to follow It—
     To what place will you go?

Know That which is beyond all beginnings
     And you will know everything right here and now
Know everything in this moment
     And you will know the Eternal Tao

Tao Te Ching
VERSE 47

Without going out the door
    one can know the whole world
Without glancing out the window
    one can see the ways of Heaven
The further one goes
    the less one knows

Thus the Sage does not go yet he knows
    He does not look yet he sees
    He does not do yet all is done

Tao Te Ching

Those who look down upon the world
 will surely take hold and try to change things
But this is a plan
 I've seen fail again and again
The world is Tao's own vessel
 It is Perfection manifest
It cannot be changed
It cannot be improved
For those who go on tampering, it's ruined
For those who try to grasp, it's gone

Allow your life to unfold naturally
Know that it too is a vessel of perfection
Just as you breathe in and breathe out
 So, sometimes you're ahead and other times behind
 Sometimes you're strong and other times weak
 Sometimes you're joined and other times alone

To the Sage
 all of life is but a movement toward perfection
So what need has he
 for the excessive, the extravagant, or the extreme?

Tao Te Ching

Again and again
Men come in with birth
    and go out with death
One in three are followers of life
One in three are followers of death
And those just passing from life to death
    also number one in three
But they all die in the end
Why is this so?
Because they all clutch to life
    and cling to this passing world

I hear that one who lives by his inner truth
    is not like this
He walks without making footprints in this world
Going about, he does not fear the rhinoceros or tiger
Entering a battlefield, he does not fear sharp weapons
For in him the rhino can find no place to pitch its horn
The tiger no place to fix its claw
The soldier no place to thrust his blade
Why is this so?
Because he dwells in that place
    where death cannot enter

Tao Te Ching ⫸
VERSE 51

Tao gives all things life
    Te gives them fulfillment
Nature is what shapes them
Living is what brings them to completion
Every creature honors Tao and worships Te
    not by force
    but by its own living and breathing

Though Tao gives all things life
    Te is what cultivates them
Te is that magic power which
    raises and rears them
    completes and prepares them
    comforts and protects them

To create without owning
To give without expecting
To fill without claiming
    This is the profound expression of Tao
    The perfect completion of Te

Tao Te Ching

When life begins
   we are tender and weak
When life ends
   we are stiff and rigid
All things—the grass, the trees—
   while living are soft and pliant
   in death are dry and brittle

So the soft and supple
   are the companions of life
While the stiff and unyielding
   are the companions of death

An army that cannot yield
   will suffer defeat
A tree that cannot bend
   will crack in the wind
Thus by Nature's own decree
   The hard and strong are defeated
   while the soft and gentle are triumphant

Tao Te Ching

Nothing in this world
    is as soft and yielding as water
Yet for attacking the hard and strong
    none can triumph so easily
It is weak, yet none can equal it
It is soft, yet none can damage it
It is yielding, yet none can wear it away

Everyone knows that the soft overcomes the hard
    and the yielding triumphs over the rigid
Why then so little faith?
Why can no one practice it?

So the Sages say—
    Fulfill even the lowest position
    Love even the weakest creature
Then you will be called
    "Lord of every offering"
    "King of all below Heaven"

Tao Te Ching ⁂

"Surrender brings perfection"

The crooked are made straight
The empty are made full
The worn are made new
 Have little and gain much
 Have much and lose your way

So the Sage embraces the One
 and comes to know the whole world
Not displaying himself, he shines forth
Not promoting himself, he is distinguished
Not claiming reward, he gains endless merit
Not wanting glory, his glory endures

The Sage knows how to follow
 so he comes to command
He does not compete
 so no one under Heaven can compete with him

The ancient saying,
 "Surrender brings perfection"
 is not just empty words
Truly, to the yielding comes the perfect
 To the perfect comes the whole Universe

Tao Te Ching ⟫

Hold fast to the Power of the One
It will unify the body
    and merge it with the spirit
It will cleanse the vision
    and reveal the world as flawless
It will focus the life-force
    and make one supple as a newborn

As you love the people and rule the state
    can you be free of self-interest?
As the gates of Heaven open and close
    can you remain steadfast as the mother bird
    who sits with her nest?
As your wisdom reaches the four corners of the world
    can you keep the innocence of a beginner?

Know this Mysterious Power—
It guides without forcing
It serves without seeking reward
It brings forth and sustains life
    yet does not own or possess it

He who holds this Power
    brings Tao to this very Earth
He can triumph over the dragon's fire
    or the freeze of winter weather
Yet when he comes to rule the world
    it's with the gentleness of a feather

Chuang Tzu

The perfect man is a spiritual being,
    not bound by flesh.
Were the oceans to boil up around him,
    he would not feel hot.
Were the cosmos to freeze up in ice,
    he would not feel cold.
Were lightning to crack open the mountains
    and fierce winds to heave the seas,
    he would not stir.

Such a being rides upon the clouds of heaven,
    mounts the sun and moon,
    and passes with ease
    beyond the reaches of this world.
Neither life nor death can touch him—
    how much less so the concern
    of gain or loss?

Chuang Tzu ≫

The Sage stands next to the Sun
   and the Moon
   while holding all of space and time
   in his hand.
He discards the confused and obscure;
   honors the meek and humble;
   and blends everything
         into a universal whole.
As men toil on to obtain some reward,
   he appears listless and dull.
For he has merged all things
   into complete purity.
And from this purity
   he can vanquish the disparities
   of ten thousand ages
   in a single moment.

On and on goes his delight;
Should the whole of creation
   come to an end,
   his delight
   would go on still.

Chuang Tzu ⚜

When Tzu-ch'i of Nan-po was taking his stroll by the Hill of Shang he spotted a great tree towering above all the rest. Its branches could shelter a thousand teams of horses and its shade would easily cover them all. "What kind of tree is this?" he thought. "Its timber must be quite extraordinary." But when looking up he discovered that the higher branches were too gnarled to be used for floorboards or rafters. When looking down he noticed that the trunk was too soft and pitted to be used for coffins. He licked one of the leaves and it left a burning taste in his mouth. He sniffed the bark and the odor was enough to take away his appetite for three days. "This wretched tree is completely useless," he thought, "and this must be why it has been able to grow so large!" Aha!—this is the exact kind of uselessness that the holy man puts to great use.

Chuang Tzu ›››

Master carpenter Ch'ing set out to carve a piece of wood into a bell stand. When the stand was completed, all those who looked at it were amazed. Surely they thought, this must be the handiwork of the gods themselves. When the Prince of Lu saw this stand he asked, "What is the secret of your art?"

"What secret?" Ch'ing replied. "I am but a simple craftsman. There is one thing, however. Before I set about carving the wood I guard against anything that will diminish my vital force. I keep all distractions at a distance and my mind becomes very still. After three days in this state, I lose all thoughts of reward or personal benefit. After five days, I no longer care about praise or blame, or of what it takes to make a good or bad stand. After seven days I lose all notion that these are my hands or that this body belongs to me. I don't even know why I am making this stand or for whom. My skill is focused on but one thing; all disturbance of the outer world is gone. It is only then that I enter the forest in search of the right tree. I find one of exquisite form. Seeing the bell stand captured within the folds of the grain, I set my hand to the chisel so as to free it. If this is not your approach, why keep everyone up at night with the banging of your chisel? So you see it is very simple: I just bring my own nature into harmony with that of the wood. What people suspect is the work of some supernatural force is no more than this."

Chuang Tzu

Confucius once returned from a visit to Lao Tzu and was asked by his disciples:

"Master, in what ways did you debate with Lao Tzu?"

Confucius replied:

"I have seen the fierce tiger caged, the great tortoise snared, even the swiftest bird felled by an arrow, yet when I visited the House of Chou I saw a dragon—a dragon by which some miracle had fashioned a body, by which blazing heat shines forth color, by which riding upon the clouds of heaven the two principles of creation are nourished. That dragon was Lao Tzu. My mouth was agape; I could not talk. Tell me, then, how was I supposed to debate with him?"

Chuang Tzu 🌾

A philosopher once came to discuss the rules of proper conduct with Lao Tzu, and he got this reply:

> If when winnowing chaff, the dust blows in your eyes, how can you find true direction? If a swarm of mosquitoes is biting you at night, how are you to get any sleep? So let me tell you, all this talk of "benevolence" and "goodness to one's neighbor" is nothing but an annoyance which only confuses the mind and keeps people up at night! Just let the world hold to its own nature. Let the wind blow as it may. And you—just follow your own nature. Surely these virtues you talk about will come and establish themselves. Wherefore this self-defeating effort, as if searching for a runaway son while beating on a loud drum?

> The swan is white without a daily bath; the crow is black without the need to color itself. Can we argue whether white is fitting for the swan or black the crow? Can fame or the learning of proper conduct add anything to the greatness which a man already possesses? When the water dries up, the fish are left on the ground with nothing but the spittle from their mouths to moisten each other—tell me, can this compare to leaving them in their own native rivers and lakes?

> Alas then—be off! Your are disturbing the nature of man with all your talk!

Chuang Tzu ⁂

Some day comes the Great Awakening
    when we realize
    that this life
    is no more than a dream,
Yet the foolish go on thinking
    they are awake.
Surveying the panorama of life
    with such clarity,
    they call this one a prince
    and that one a peasant—
What delusion!
The great Confucius and you
    are both a dream.
And I, who say all this is a dream,
    I, too, am a dream.

What mystery this vision contains!

Someday a great Sage will come
    and explain it to us,
But that may not be
    until ten thousand generations
    have passed by.
Still, for us in this dream,
    it will only seem
    like the passing
    of a single morning or afternoon.

Lieḥ Tzu ⇒»

When Yin Sheng heard of Lieh Tzu's ability to ride on the wings of the wind, he immediately set off to become his disciple. After only a few days with the Sage, Yin Sheng pleaded for initiation into the secret arts. Ten times he asked, and ten times he received no answer. Yin Sheng finally lost his patience and went to bid the Master farewell. Lieh Tzu said to him:

> Why this impatience? Why all this coming and going? Sit down already and I will tell you something about my own Master. After I had served him for three years, my mind was calm and no longer reflected on right and wrong, my lips were still and no longer spoke of gain or loss. Then, for the first time, my Master glanced at me—nothing more.
>
> After five years of service, something shifted: my mind was filled with thoughts of right and wrong, and my lips kept talking about gain and loss. Then, for the first time, my Master's face softened and he smiled at me.
>
> After seven years of service there was another shift: I let my mind entertain what thoughts it may, but it no longer had thoughts of right and wrong. I let my lips talk about whatever they wanted to, but there was not another word about gain or loss. Then, and only then, my Master asked me to come sit by his side.
>
> After nine years of service my mind merged back into its own source, my lips spoke only words of truth. I knew nothing about right and wrong, gain or loss. I knew nothing about Master and disciple—for I could no longer tell the difference. Inside and outside had merged into One. No longer was there a distinction between eye and ear, ear and nose, nose and mouth—all were the same. My mind was silent, my body had dissolved; my flesh and my bones melted into nothingness. I was totally unaware of having a body, or what was under my feet. Suddenly I was carried up by the hands of the wind—flying this way and that—like dry chaff or a

falling leaf. I floated up through the skies not knowing whether I was riding the wind or whether the wind was riding me!

One day, Yin Sheng, you too will learn how to fly, but first you must learn how to stay in one place on this earth.

The Buddhist Masters

THE SANSKRIT WORD *BUDDHA* MEANS "THE AWAK-
ened One," and Buddhism was born of the final awakening of
Shakyamuni Buddha (?563—?483 B.C.), also known as Siddhartha
Gautama. The fundamental tenet put forth by the Buddha is that
life (separate existence) brings suffering, that suffering has its roots
in desire, and that by systematic practice desire can be destroyed
and Nirvana—a state of bliss beyond all suffering—can be reached.

The Buddha was born as a prince of the Shakyas in a small
kingdom at the foot of the Himalayas. As prince, he lived a privi-
leged and sheltered life where all his needs were met and all his desires fulfilled. One day he ventured beyond the high walls of the
palace, where he witnessed death, sickness, and the suffering of the
world. Deeply troubled by what he saw, Siddhartha soon left his
comfortable surroundings and set out to find the way to overcome
this suffering. After years of meditation and severe austerities he
attained enlightenment under the now famed *bodhi* (enlightenment) tree.

A small Buddhist canon attributed to the Buddha is the
Dhammapada, a brilliant collection of short and penetrating
verses that gives the essence of Buddha's teachings.

A Chinese Zen Master and a forefather of the Rinzai school
of Zen was **Huang Po** (d. 850). Zen Buddhism stresses the importance of enlightenment and the practice of knowing one's own
mind through the practice of *zazen*, thought-free meditation. The
Rinzai school stresses the use of a *koan*—a riddle which cannot be
answered by the intellect—to bring the student beyond the mind
into a state of sudden realization. Huang Po's lasting contribution
was his non-dual philosophy called "Doctrine of the One Mind."

The Chinese Master **Yoka Daishi** (665–713) was said to
have been in a state of perfect repose while walking, standing, sitting, and lying down. According to legend, he visited the great Zen

Patriarch Hui-neng and attained complete realization in one night; and so he was called "master of the enlightenment attained in one night."

Shantideva (7th century) was a Master of Mahayana Buddhism ("The Great Vehicle"), a school which emphasizes enlightenment not for the individual's sake, but for the benefit of all mankind. In his book *Entering the Path of Enlightenment*, he describes two practices of meditation: cultivating equality consciousness and seeing oneself in all others.

The most important Zen Master, and considered Japan's "greatest religious figure," was **Eihei Dogen** (1200–1253). He was the founder of the Soto school, whose emphasis is on gradual enlightenment through the practice of pure meditation called *shikan-taza*, an alert, thought-free state of awareness, sometimes called "the mind of someone facing death."

Two other Japanese Zen Masters were **Bassui Zenji** (1327–1387) and **Gizan** (1802–1878). At an early age Bassui began to question his own nature, and he soon set out to find a Master. During his search he never stayed overnight in a temple but rather made his home in some isolated hut where he would practice *zazen* hour after hour and ponder his own natural *koan*, "who is the Master?" Finally he met the Master Koho Zenji and reached enlightenment. Gizan was a lesser-known Zen Master whose decisive poetry and bold teaching style endeared him to all his followers.

The Buddha ⁂
THE POWER OF FAITH

Siddhartha was tempted by the illusive power of Maya
    and replied:

Why do you tempt me, Maya?
What will I do with all the pleasures you offer,
I who have faith?
    I am established in faith, evil one;
      My faith is my life.
My faith, like a burning wind
    that dries up rivers,
    will dry up my blood
    and everything that flows.
Till blood, bile, and phlegm dry up,
I shall sit here,
    with a tranquil mind
    and steady wisdom.

Faith is my weapon, O Temptress.
Your army is powerless against it.
Bring Lust and Restlessness,
Hunger and Thirst,
Sloth, Cowardice, Doubt, and Hypocrisy—
All powerless.

The Buddha ⁓
MY TEACHINGS

Consider carefully the things I have taught and the things I have not taught.

I have not taught that the world is eternal. I have not taught that the world is ephemeral. I have not taught that the world is finite. I have not taught that the world is infinite. I have not taught that the soul and the body are the same. I have not taught that the soul and the body are different. I have not taught that the liberated person exists after death. I have not taught that he does not exist after death . . .

Why have I not taught all this? Because all this is useless, it has nothing to do with real Truth. It does not lead to cessation of passion, to peace, to supreme wisdom, to the holy life, nor to Nirvana. That is why I have not taught all this.

And what have I taught? I have taught that suffering exists, that suffering has an origin, that suffering has an end.

Why have I taught this? Because this is useful, it has to do with real Truth. It leads to the cessation of passion, it brings peace, supreme wisdom, the holy life, and Nirvana. That is why I have taught all this.

Therefore, consider carefully what I have taught and what I have not taught.

Dhammapada

The mind—
This is the beginning and the end of it all.
The quality of one's life depends on
    nothing but the mind.
If one's words or deeds come from an impure mind,
    then suffering will follow.
If one's words and deeds come from a pure mind,
    then happiness walks with him as his own shadow.

How can such thoughts as,
"He abused me, he cheated me, he robbed me,"
    release one from the snares of anger?
Hatred is never banished by hatred.
Hatred is only banished by love.
This is a law that will never change.

We are guests in this world,
    here for only a short while.
Those who know this truth do not waste their time
    with quibbling or gossip.

Living only for pleasure,
    stuffing oneself with this and that,
    being lazy and undisciplined—
This makes one powerless.
Maya's illusion blows him about
    like a twig blown about in a storm.

One who chooses the beneficial over the pleasurable,
Who has his senses under control,
Who has faith and puts forth effort—
He is a mountain
That stands unshaken by the winds of this world . . .

As rain seeps through a poorly thatched roof,
Passion seeps through a poorly trained mind.
As rain is held back by a well-thatched roof,
Passion is held back by a well-trained mind.

One who knows the scriptures
But does not live by them
Does not share in the bounty of a holy life.
He is like the cowherd
Who counts someone else's cattle.
One who knows a few lines from the scriptures
And lives by them—
    Harboring only good thoughts,
    Banishing hatred and delusion,
    Wanting nothing from this world or the next—
He reaps the full bounty of a holy life.

Dhammapada

THE SAINT

His journey is over,
All sorrow is gone,
Every shackle undone;
He is completely free.

One who yearns to be free
    is not content to remain in one place.
He is ever-striving for a way
    to pass beyond this world,
    like a swan leaving its lake
    to fly upwards to the sky.

Who can trace the path of these great ones?
These beings who are pure at heart,
    not swayed by the senses,
    living without attachment,
    accepting of whatever life gives them?

More difficult than following the flight of birds
    is following these beings,
    these great ones who
    wander through the infinite skies
    with absolute freedom.

Even the gods envy them.
Their senses are controlled like a well-trained horse,
Their souls are free of pride and jealousy.
These great beings welcome everyone like the earth.
They are steadfast like a stone foundation,
Pure like the waters of a lake,
And no longer bound by birth or death.
Perfect wisdom has filled them with peace.

Their every thought, word, and action
   are in perfect harmony with the universe.

Having seen the Eternal Truth
All falsehood has vanished,
All bonds have been cut,
All desires have been conquered . . .
They are, indeed, the kings among men.

Dhammapada
THE THOUSANDS

Better than a thousand useless words
Is one word that brings peace.
Better than a thousand useless verses
Is one line that brings joy.
Better than a thousand useless poems
Is one poem that brings love.

One day of contemplation
Is better than a hundred years of thoughtlessness.
One day of wisdom
Is better than a hundred years of ignorance.
One day of effort
Is better than a hundred years of laziness.

One moment of reverence for a Master
Is better than a hundred years of worship
     and a thousand sacred rituals.

One moment of reverence for a Master
Is better than living in the forest a hundred years
     and tending a thousand sacrificial fires.

One moment of reverence for a Master
Is better than one hundred years of
     beauty, happiness, and strength.

Eihei Dogen
THE RIGHT BEGINNING

A teacher of old said, "If the beginning is not right, a thousand practices will be useless."

How true these words are! Practice of the way depends on whether the guiding master is a true teacher or not.

The disciple is like wood, and the teacher resembles a craftsman. Even if the wood is good, without a skilled craftsman its extraordinary beauty is not revealed. Even if the wood is bent, placed in skilled hands its splendid merits immediately appear. By this you should know that realization is genuine or false depending on whether the teacher is true or incompetent.

Bassui Zenji ﷽
REALIZING THE MIND

If you would free yourself from the sufferings of birth and death, you must learn the direct way to become a Buddha. This way is no other than the realization of your own Mind . . . If you want to realize your own Mind, you must first of all look into the source from which thoughts flow. Sleeping and working, standing and sitting, profoundly ask yourself, "What is my own Mind," with an intense yearning to resolve this question. This searching of one's own Mind leads ultimately to enlightenment.

Bassui Zenji ﷽
WAKEFULNESS

Imagine a child sleeping next to its parents and dreaming it is being beaten or is painfully sick. The parents cannot help the child no matter how much it suffers . . . If the child could awaken itself, it could be freed of this suffering automatically. In the same way, one who realizes that his own Mind is Buddha frees himself instantly from sufferings arising from the ceaseless change of birth-and-death. If a Buddha could prevent it, do you think he would allow even one sentient being to fall into hell?

What is obstructing realization? Nothing but your own half-hearted desire for truth. Think of this and exert yourself to the utmost.

Huang Po
DOCTRINE OF THE ONE MIND

All the Buddhas and all sentient beings are nothing but the Universal Mind, beside which nothing exists. This Mind, which is without beginning, is unborn and indestructible. It is not green nor yellow, and has neither form nor appearance. It does not belong to the categories of things which exist or do not exist, nor can it be thought of in terms of new or old. It is neither long nor short, big nor small, for it transcends all limits, measures, traces, and comparisons.

The Universal Mind alone is the Buddha and there is no distinction between the Buddha and sentient beings, but sentient beings are attached to forms and so seek externally for Buddhahood. By their very seeking for it they lose it . . . If they could only put a stop to their conceptual thoughts they would realize that the Buddha is directly before them . . .

Countless as the sands of the Ganges are the merits which come from performing the six perfect duties and vast number of similar practices. But since you are fundamentally complete in every respect, you should not try to supplement that perfection by such meaningless practices. When there is occasion for them, perform them, and when the occasion has passed, remain quiescent. If you are not absolutely convinced that the Mind is the Buddha, and if you are attached to forms, practices, and meritorious deeds, your way of thinking is false and quite contrary to the Way. Your mind is the Buddha! There is no other Buddha! There is no other Mind!

Huang Po ⫸
BUDDHA-NATURE

Our original Buddha-Nature is, in highest truth, devoid of any trace of objectivity. It is void, omnipresent, silent, pure; it is glorious and mysterious peaceful joy—and that is all. Enter deeply in it by awakening to it yourself. That which is before you is it, in all its fullness, utterly complete. There is naught besides. Even if you go through all the stages of a Bodhisattva's progress toward Buddhahood, one by one, when at last, in a single flash, you attain to full realization, you will only be realizing the Buddha-Nature that has been with you all the time; and by all the foregoing stages you will have added to it nothing at all. You will come to look upon those aeons of work and achievement as no better than unreal actions performed in a dream. That is why the Tathagata [the Buddha] said: "I truly attained nothing from complete, unexcelled Enlightenment."

Shantideva ⫸
THE PAIN THAT WINS ENLIGHTENMENT

The pain that wins me Enlightenment is of brief term; it is like the pain of cutting out a buried arrow to heal its smart. All physicians restore health by painful courses; then to undo much suffering let us bear a little. But even this fitting course the Great Physician has not enjoined upon us: he heals those who are grievously sick by the most tender treatment.

Yoka Daishi ⫸

One Nature,
  perfect and pervading,
  circulates in all natures.
One Reality,
  all comprehensive,
  contains within itself all realities.
The one moon is reflected
  wherever there is a sheet of water,
And all the moons in all the waters
  are embraced within the one moon;
The embodied Truth of all the Buddhas
  enters into my own being,
And my own being is found in union with theirs.

"No" is not necessarily "no," nor is "yes" necessarily "yes."
But when you miss even a tenth of an inch,
  the difference widens up to a thousand miles.
When it is "yes,"
  a young native girl attains Buddhahood in an instant.
When it is "no,"
  the greatest living scholar falls into hell.

Gizan ⚜

Coming and going,
  life and death.
A thousand villages,
  a million houses.
Don't you get it?—
Moon in the water,
  blossom in the sky.

Wisdom of the Hebrews

THE HEBREW SCRIPTURES ARE AN EXTENSIVE BODY of literature that trace the early history and spiritual unfolding of a small but determined people. The genius of these early Hebrew sages, and the sweeping expression of their religious zeal, colors every page of this exalted work. The most familiar and widely used book of the Bible is *The Book of Psalms* (10th–3rd centuries B.C.); it is a collection of sacred songs which has been aptly called "the immortal song-book of the human heart." Through its 150 hymns it captures the feeling and spirit of the Old Testament: tracing Jewish history, giving the essential teachings of the prophets, honoring the Law, and running the gamut of religious feeling—from anguish and despair to devotion, faith, and love for God. Because of its rich spirituality and depth of religious feeling, the Psalms are embraced by all people and form a common ground for the Jewish and Christian faiths. Although the authors of the Psalms are unknown, about half the songs are attributed to King David.

Five books of the Bible—Proverbs, Ecclesiastes, Job, The Wisdom of Solomon, and Ecclesiasticus (The Wisdom of Sirach)—make up what is known as the Wisdom Literature. This is a group of writings filled with pithy sayings, universal teachings, spiritual insights, and praises of the creative power of God known as *Sophia*, Wisdom. *Ecclesiasticus* (180 B.C.) was written in Hebrew by Jeshua ben Sirach of Jerusalem. Its ethical outlook, wit, keen observation, and use of parallel couplets give it a close resemblance to Proverbs. *The Wisdom of Solomon* (?50 B.C.) was written in Greek by an unknown Jewish sage living in Alexandria. It offers a true fusion of Greek and Jewish ideas. By custom, however, it is ascribed to King Solomon (10th century B.C.).

Both Ecclesiasticus and The Wisdom of Solomon are found in a portion of the Bible called the *Apocrypha*, a Greek word meaning "hidden" or "obscure"—a word which later came to mean "dubious" or "unauthorized." Although of Jewish origin, the writings of the Apocrypha were rejected as part of the Jewish canon because of their late date—written during the interval between the end of the Old Testament and the beginning of the New Testament—and also because the authors of the writings do not claim Divine Revelation as their source. The Roman Catholic Church, however, judged these writings to be valid and included them in its official Bible, placed between the Old and New Testaments. The King James Version of 1611 also includes this "hidden" portion.

The Apocrypha give a brilliant, personal, and poetic account of God's feminine aspect. This creative power, supreme intelligence, and wisdom inherent in man was called *Shekinah* by the Jewish mystics, and to the Greeks of a later time, She became *Sophia*, their word for "wisdom." In these books *Sophia* is described as "pervading and permeating all things," and as "the source of all treasure in the universe." In one of the verses She herself says: "Every people and nation are under my sway." It may be that these Wisdom books were banned from the Jewish canon not because they lacked divine inspiration but because of the danger that this Supreme Female Spirit—which is the active or creative aspect of the One God—might be viewed as a second and separate Divinity, and threaten the monistic foundation upon which Judaism is based.

Psalm 23

The Lord is my shepherd;
I shall not want.
He brings me to where the grass is green
    and leads me to where the waters are still.
I drink—and I am filled with life!

All I do is call out His Name
    and the right path appears before me.
Even though I walk through this world,
    where the shadow of death falls on everyone,
I fear no harm—
    for He is always with me,
    His staff is always ready to protect me.
In this place filled with hunger
    the Lord has spread out a table of delights
    and bathed my head in scented oil.

My heart is filled with His Love;
Goodness and Purity will follow me
    every day of my life.

Although appearing like others,
    I do not live in this world of men:
I live in the Lord's house,
    I am forever in His keeping.

Psalm 119 ⟫

A LEPH ◆

Blessed are those whose way is pure,
>   who walk the path you have shown them.
Blessed are those who hear your voice,
>   who seek you with all their hearts.
I pray that my life pleases you,
>   that it be lived according to your ways.

B ETH ◆

How can my actions be true and pure?—
>   by keeping them in accordance with your will.
With all my heart I have longed for you—
>   do not let me wander
>   from the truth you have shown me.

Through your word I have found a treasure in my heart.
Through your word my every sin has vanished . . .

With my lips I have sung your glory.
I have rejoiced in your teachings
>   as much as in all the world's riches.
I have imbibed your way—the way of my own heart.
O Lord, my delight is boundless
>   now that your Name has become my own.

D ALETH ◆

My soul cleaves to the dust;
>   my eyes stare into the dark of night.
O giver of life!—
I have prayed and you have answered;
I have wept and you have given me strength.
O Lord, remove the darkness from my soul
>   and show me the light of your truth.

V A V ◆

May your love and kindness find shelter
    in the depths of my heart.
May your word be my salvation.
O Lord, do not take the truth from my lips;
    keep it with me
        so that I may sing your glory forever.

I walk freely, speaking to all who seek your wisdom;
I tell of your miracle to kings and princes,
    and I am not daunted.
I delight in your wisdom,
I reach out my hand for your touch,
    and I hold on to your every word.
How great is my fortune,
How great are the gifts that come from you.

Z A Y I N ◆

O Lord, hear the call of your servant:
Your Name has given me hope;
    it is my comfort in affliction.
Your Name has given me new life.
Your boundless glory
    is the song I sing in every house;
The remembrance of your Name is the truth I keep each night
    as I lie down to sleep.

H E T H ◆

O Lord, your giving is complete;
    there is nothing more I want.
I have promised to do as you bid me,
And your grace unfolds within my heart.
O Lord, I am gone; you have become my everything.

YODH ◆

Your hands fashioned me;
    show me the truth
    and the wisdom to know your will.
Let the people who love you, see me and be glad;
    for they will know that I am your messenger,
    that I come to speak your words.

O Lord, I know that every hardship along the way
    allows me to grow in your love.
May I find delight in all you offer.
May I comfort all those who turn in my direction.
May my joy be complete
    and your Name forever on my lips.

KAPH ◆

My soul longs to know you again.
I stand here hoping for a sign,
    hoping for a thread to grasp . . .
My sight has grown dim searching for you.
When will you come?
When will you show yourself to me?
I may shrivel up like a wineskin,
I may be hounded by vicious lies,
I may be swept from this earth,
    but I will never turn away from you.
What was I born for, if not to follow you?
What is there to live for, if not your undying love?
O Lord, come alive in my heart—
Come alive so that we may, once again,
    be as one.

LAMED ◆

O Lord, your Word is eternal;
It is fixed in the heavens,
It stands as firm as the earth,
It has fulfilled the prayers of every generation.

O Lord, without the strength that comes
    from your Name
    I would have perished long ago.

I will never forget your teachings,
    for they have made you come alive within me.
I may see the heavens fall,
I may see the earth crumble,
I may see all creation come to an end,
    but I will stand here, forever,
    as your servant.

M E M   ◆
O Lord, I hold your love with me all the time.
It makes me strong.
It cuts through my doubts.
It gives me insight
    and the wisdom of a sage.
It keeps me on the right path.
How sweet is your love to my taste,
    sweeter than honey to my lips!
O Lord, what is there without your love?—
Without your love there is nothing
    but the taste of bitterness.

N U N   ◆
O Lord, you are a lamp to my feet,
    a shining light on my path.
Wherever you go, there I have sworn to follow.
I know the way may be steep,
    and the journey filled with pain,
    but every step of the way
    you will give me strength.
O Lord, how can I ever hope to repay you?
You are my everlasting inheritance,
    you are the joy of my life.

I stand here resolved,
    ready to take my heart
    on the path that leads me back to you.

S A M E K ◆
You are my shield and my hiding place.
You are my sole protector.
You are my only support.
O Lord, banish all evil from my mind
    and replace it with the yearning to know you.
Give me faith and humility
    and keep me free from harm.
What use is this life without you?
You are all that is safe,
    and all that is true.

A Y I N ◆
All my life I have looked for you.
Could you let these eyes fail
    before they have rested upon your form?
Could you forsake me in that way?
O Lord, be kind to your servant—
    show yourself to me.
This is my truth, this is my life,
    this is what I want more
    than all the world has to offer.

P E ◆
Every word that comes from your lips
    fills me with wonder.
And here I sit, waiting to fulfill your every word.
Your words shine;
    they illumine those in despair;
    they give understanding to the simple.
I am out of breath calling for you . . .
Turn in my direction
    and fill me with your grace.

I am knocking—open the door:
    for this is the promise
    you have given to all those who love you.
O Lord, fulfill your promise—
    keep my feet on the path that leads to your glory.
Do not let anything take me away.
Let the glory of your splendor
    be seen by this servant of yours . . .
If I go my own way
    and do not follow your laws
    then let me suffer,
    let me wail,
    let my eyes rain down with a flood of tears.

T s a d h e ◆
O Lord, I have no doubt—
    you are all that is just,
    you are all that is true.
This whole world is a gift from you.

Your Word is taintless,
    it never fails in its giving.
Though I am small and of little account,
    I always repeat your Name,
    I always remember your Truth,
    I always fill myself with your eternal love.
O Lord, what else can you give?
You have given me the truth of the universe,
    you have given me my very breath.

Q u o p h ◆
I cry out with my whole heart. O Lord—answer me!
Save me from this ocean of darkness.
Show me the way out.
I rise before dawn and wait to hear your voice.

My eyes stay open past the midnight watch,
    that I might understand all you have taught me.

You are so near, my Lord.
    You are the eternal support.
    You are the Supreme goal . . .
I have but one prayer:
    that every step I take
    be a step toward you.

S H I N   ◆
My heart stands in awe of you,
    and I am filled with joy whenever I hear your Name.
Seven times a day I praise you;
    seven times a day I remember the justice of your care.
Those who love everything you give
    find great peace
    and nothing causes them to stumble.
Here I am, do with me as you will,
    for all my life lies open before you.

T A V   ◆
Let my tears reach you,
    let my worship be seen by you.
Let my tongue sing of your glory,
    and let my life be a testimony of your compassion . . .

O Lord, where is my salvation?
Where is this life bringing me?
If I go astray, like a lost sheep, look for me.

Look for me, O Lord!
For I am your servant—
    I am the one who will never forget you,
    I am the one who will hold your love forever.

The Wisdom of Solomon

SOPHIA

Sophia is the Supreme Spirit devoted to the good of all people . . .

She shines bright in the gloom of ignorance;
She is unfading;
    She is easily seen by those who love Her;
    easily found by those who look for Her,
And quickly does She come
    to those who seek Her help.

One who rises early,
    intent on finding Her,
    will not grow weary of the quest—
For one day he will find Her seated in his own heart.

To set all one's thoughts on Her
    is true wisdom,
And to be ever aware of Her
    is the sure way to perfect peace.
For *Sophia* Herself goes about in search
    of those who are worthy of Her.
With every step She comes to guide them;
    in every thought She comes to meet them . . .

The true beginning of spiritual life is the desire to know *Sophia*.
A desire to know Her brings one to love Her.
Loving Her enables one to follow Her will.
Following Her will is the sure path to immortality.
And immortality is oneness with God.
So the desire to know *Sophia*
    leads to God and His Kingdom—
    a never-fading Kingdom.
With all your thrones and scepters
    you may rule the world for a while,
But take hold of *Sophia*
    and you will rule the world forever.

The Wisdom of Solomon

SOPHIA

I, too, am a mortal man, like all of you,
Descended from the fist born,
Formed out of the earth in
　　my mother's womb . . .
When I was born, I breathed in the common air,
　　was laid upon this earth,
　　and wailed out a cry as all others do.
No king begins life in any other way;
For everyone comes into this world by one path
　　and by the same path they go out again.

Seeing this predicament, I prayed,
　　and wisdom was given to me;
I called for help,
　　and the Supreme Spirit, *Sophia*,
　　answered me.
I valued Her above scepter and throne . . .
Next to Her, all the gold in the world
　　seemed like a handful of sand,
　　and all the silver like a pile of dirt.
I loved Her more than health and beauty,
　　and preferred Her to the light of day.
For Her radiance never fades
　　and Her light never sets.

With Her comes all good things,
　　and She carries in Her arms
　　wealth past counting.
I rejoiced with love for all people,
　　as I could see *Sophia* in their hearts,
　　guiding them.

What I learned with great effort
    I now share freely;
    I do not hoard Her wealth for myself.
She is an inexhaustible treasure for mankind;
She blesses the world with Supreme wisdom,
    and allows all people to realize
    their unity with God.

She is the Supreme Spirit:
All-knowing and sacred;
One, yet pervading many,
    subtle, ever-free, lucid,
    stainless, clear, and invincible.
She is the love of goodness,
    ever-ready, unobstructed,
    beneficent, kindly toward all,
    steadfast, unerring, and untouched by care.
She is all-powerful, the witness of all,
    and found in those
    who are wise, pure-hearted, and humble.

Sophia moves more easily than motion itself;
By reason of Her purity
    She permeates all things.
She is like a fine mist
    rising from the power of God,
The divine radiance
    streaming from the glory of the Almighty.
Nothing can stain Her immaculate purity.
She is the shimmering glow of everlasting Light,
The flawless mirror of God's Power on earth,
The supreme image of all good things.

Though one, She becomes everything;
    from within Herself, by Her own power,
She makes all things new.

Age after age She enters into holy souls,
    making them perfect,
    and leading them back to God.
For God only accepts those
    who have made their home with *Sophia*.
She is fairer than the sun,
    and greater than every constellation.
She is more radiant than the light of day—
    for day is overcome by night,
    but against *Sophia* no darkness can prevail.

The Wisdom of Solomon ⤜

SOPHIA

Sophia I loved;
I sought Her out in my youth,
I fell in love with Her beauty,
    and I longed to make Her my bride.
All glory is born of Her,
    for She is one with God;
The Lord of all things
    loves Her as Himself.
She is the Supreme Power of initiation,
    imparting the secret knowledge of God,
    and carrying out all His works.
If wealth is desired,
    what wealth could be greater than *Sophia*,
    the source of all treasure in the universe?

But I saw that my efforts were useless:
Only through the gift of God
    could I have Her for my own.
My understanding was such
    that I knew at least this much.
And so I pleaded with the Lord,
    and prayed from the deepest reaches of my heart:

    O Lord, God of our Fathers,
    Whose Word has made all things,
    Whose wisdom fills every heart with righteousness;
    O Lord, O merciful Lord,
    Grant me that One who sits by your throne—
    Grant me Sophia.

Ecclesiasticus (Sirach) ⋙

Hear the praise of *Sophia* from Her own mouth:

"I am the word which was spoken by the Most High;
it was I who covered the earth like a mist.
My dwelling-place was in high heaven;
my throne was in a pillar of cloud.
Alone I made a circuit of the sky
and traversed the depth of the abyss.
The waves of the sea, the whole earth,
every people and nation are under my sway . . .
Before time began He created me,
and I shall remain for ever.
In the sacred tent I ministered in His presence,
and so I came to be established in Zion.
Thus He settled me in the city He loved
and gave me authority in Jerusalem.
I took root among the people whom the Lord has honoured
by choosing them to be His special possession.
There I grew like cedar of Lebanon,
like the cypress on the slopes of Hermon,
like the date-palms at Engedi,
like roses at Jericho.
I grew like a fair olive-tree in the vale,
or like a plane-tree planted beside the water.
Like cassia or camel-thorn I was redolent of spices;
I spread my fragrance like choice myrrh . . .
I was like the smoke of incense in the sacred tent.
Like terebinth I spread out my branches,
laden with honour and grace.
I put forth lovely shoots like the vine,
and my blossoms were a harvest of wealth and honour.

Come to me, you who desire me,
and eat your fill of my fruit.
The memory of me is sweeter than syrup,
the possession of me sweeter than honey dripping from the
    comb.
Whoever feeds on me will be hungry for more,
and whoever drinks from me will thirst for more.
To obey me is to be safe from disgrace;
those who work in wisdom will not go astray."

Ecclesiasticus (Sirach) ≫

All wisdom is from the Lord,
wisdom is with him for ever.
Who can count the sands of the sea,
the drops of rain, or the days of unending time?
Who can measure the height of the sky,
the breadth of the earth, or the depth of the abyss?
Wisdom was the first of all created things;
intelligent purpose has been there from the beginning.
Who has laid bare the root of wisdom?
Who has understood her subtlety?
One alone is wise, the Lord most terrible,
seated upon his throne.
It is he who created her, surveyed and measured her,
and infused her into all his works.
To all mankind, he has given her in some measure,
but in plenty to those who love him.

Wisdom raises her sons to greatness
and cares for those who seek her.
To love her is to love life;
To rise early for her sake is to be filled with joy . . .
The Lord's blessing rests upon every place she enters.

Ecclesiasticus (Sirach) ⫸

If you discover a wise man,
rise early to visit him;
let your feet wear out his doorstep . . .

Listen, my son, accept my judgement;
do not reject my advice.
Put your feet in wisdom's fetters
and your neck into her collar.
Stoop to carry her on your shoulders
and do not chafe at her bonds.
Come to her wholeheartedly,
and keep to her ways with all your might.
Follow her track, and she will make herself known to you;
once you have grasped her, never let her go.
In the end you will find the relief she offers;
she will transform herself into joy for you.
Her fetters will become your strong defense
and her collar a gorgeous robe.

The Stoic Philosophers

STOICISM BEGAN IN 310 B.C. AND GETS ITS NAME FROM *stoa*, meaning "the porch," the place in Athens where its founder, Zeno, gave his discourses. Zeno's aim was to disseminate the teachings of the great philosophers—Plato, Aristotle, Pythagoras, and Heraclitus—which for so long had been the sole property of the learned class.

The Stoics viewed God as the living universe, the Supreme Intelligence that held everything in order; and they saw a spark of this divine power in everyone. Although the Stoics insisted that there was only one supreme power, they saw it as having many aspects and they referred to each aspect by a different name—Nature, Providence, Law, Destiny, Zeus.

The most famous Stoic was **Marcus Aurelius** (A.D. 121–180), the last of the great Roman Emperors. A small journal he kept toward the end of his life, which is now entitled *The Meditations*, has done more to make Stoicism known to the world than any other work. Paradoxically, Marcus did not always fit the mold of a true Stoic—for a true Stoic was steadfast, unflinching, and indifferent to the pains and pleasures of life. Marcus, however, was endearingly mortal. He struggled with life. His *Meditations* are not written with staunch certainty but with the thoughtfulness of one still searching; they are not written with severity but with generosity and a concern about the welfare of others. Instead of going against the problems of one's life, Marcus urged himself to accept his life, and to love his destiny. Entries in his journal read, "It is said: 'Face the stormy winds that blow from God with steady oars and uncomplaining hearts.'" And again, "Love that which is woven into the pattern of your destiny—what could be better suited for your growth?" Although his journal is written to himself, we feel as if he is talking to us. His words are filled with such intimacy and sincerity that we forget he is a Roman Emperor and we feel as if we are in the company of an old and reliable friend.

In the Piazza del Campidoglio in Rome stands a statue of Marcus Aurelius of which Henry James once wrote: "In the capital of Christendom, the portrait most suggestive of a Christian conscience is that of a pagan Emperor."

Another noble Stoic was **Lucius Annaeus Seneca** (4 B.C.– A.D. 65), a brilliant Roman statesman and tragic playwright whose work influenced much of Elizabethan drama. He was a staunch humanitarian, calling hatred "the most dangerous, outrageous, brutal, and intractable of all passions." It can readily be seen why his ideas and writings were embraced by Martin Luther King and the leaders of other pacifist movements.

Epictetus (1st century A.D.) was born in Greece yet spent most of his life as a Roman slave. Whereas Marcus Aurelius wrote about Nature and the Supreme Intelligence, and Seneca about social issues, Epictetus—bearing the mark of his difficult life— stressed complete dispassion toward outer circumstances and the need to find happiness within oneself. His single volume of writing is called *The Golden Sayings of Epictetus*.

Marcus Aurelius ⁂
THE BIDDING OF NATURE

At daybreak, when you loathe the idea of having to leave your bed, have this thought ready in your mind: "I am rising for the work of man." Should I have misgivings about doing that for which I was born, and for the sake of which I came into this world? Is this the grand purpose of my existence—to lie here snug and warm underneath my blanket? Certainly it feels more pleasant. Was it for pleasure that you were made, and not for work, nor for effort? Look at the plants, sparrows, ants, spiders, and bees, all working busily away, each doing its part in welding an orderly Universe. So who are you to go against the bidding of Nature? Who are you to refuse man his share of the work?

To live each day as though it were your last—never flustered, never lazy, never a false word—herein lies the perfection of character.

Marcus Aurelius ≫

I'LL DO IT TOMORROW

Think of all the years passed by in which you said to yourself, "I'll do it tomorrow," and how the gods have again and again granted you periods of grace to which you have not availed yourself. It is time to realize that you are a member of the Universe, that you are born of Nature itself, and to know that a limit has been set to your time. Use every moment wisely, to perceive your inner refulgence, or 'twill be gone and nevermore within your reach.

In a man's life, his time is but a moment, his being a mere flux, his senses a dim glimpse, his body food for the worms, and his soul a restless eddy . . . the things of the body pass like a flowing stream; life is a brief sojourn, and one's mark in this world is soon forgotten.

Marcus Aurelius ≫
A PART OF THE WHOLE

Constantly remind yourself, "I am a member of the whole body of conscious things." If you think of yourself as a mere "part," then love for mankind will not well up in your heart; you will look for some reward in every act of kindness and miss the boon which the act itself is offering. Then all your work will be seen as a mere duty and not as the very portal connecting you with the Universe itself.

Men may block your path, but never let them obstruct you from right action, never let them destroy the feeling of charity you have toward them. You must be firm in both: steadfast in judgement and action, kind to those who do you harm. To lose your temper with them is no less a sign of weakness than one cowed into abandoning his proper course of action. In both cases, the post of duty has been deserted.

As Marcus, I have Rome; as a human being, I have the Universe. What brings benefit to these communities, that alone is what brings benefit to me.

Marcus Aurelius ❧
THE MIRACLE OF NATURE

Is your cucumber bitter?—throw it away. Are there briars in your path?—turn aside. This is enough. Do not harbor the thought "Why have such things been brought into the world?" A man of true wisdom would only laugh at you, just as a carpenter would laugh at you if you found fault with the shavings lying about his shop. The carpenter, at least, has a place to throw out his scraps; yet Nature has no such place outside Herself. And this is the miracle of Her workmanship: though limited to Herself, She takes back everything that is old, worn out, and useless, and from within Herself brings forth a new creation. She requires neither a substance outside Herself, nor a place to discard the waste: Her own space, Her own material, and Her own workmanship are sufficient unto Her.

Marcus Aurelius ❧
TRUE GIVING

There is one type of person who, whenever he does a kind deed, will not hesitate to ask for some reward. Another type of person, though not so bold, will keep track of everything he has done for you, feeling deep down that you are in his debt. Then there are those who give without any remembrance of what they have done. They are like the vine that has brought forth a cluster of grapes, and once having borne its delicious fruit, seeks nothing more. As the horse that runs its race, the hound that tracks its game, and the bee that hives its honey, so should a man be when he has done an act of kindness: not seeking reward nor proclaiming his virtues but passing on to the next act as the vine passes on to bear another cluster of summer grapes.

Marcus Aurelius ⁂

It is possible to live out your whole life in perfect contentment, even though the whole world deafens you with its roar and wild beasts tear apart your body like a lump of clay. For nothing can shake a steady mind out of its peaceful repose; nothing can bar it from correct judgement, nor defeat its readiness to see the benefit that all things bring. True understanding is to see the events of life in this way: "You are here for my benefit, though rumor paints you otherwise." And everything is turned to one's advantage when he greets a situation like this: "You are the very thing I was looking for." Truly, whatever arises in life is the right material to bring about your growth and the growth of those around you. This, in a word, is *art*—and this art we call "life" is a practice suitable to both men and gods. Everything contains some special purpose and a hidden blessing. What then could be strange or arduous when all of life is here to greet you like an old and faithful friend?

Marcus Aurelius ✹
THE HIDDEN POWER

Remember that the Hidden Power within us pulls the strings; there is the guiding force, there is the life, there, one might say, is the man himself. Never think of yourself as a mere body with its various appendages; the body is like the ax of a carpenter: dare we think that the ax is the carpenter himself? Without this Inner Cause, which dictates both action and inaction, the body is of no more use than the weaver's shuttle without a weaver, the writer's pen without a writer, or the coachman's whip without a horse and carriage.

Honor the highest thing in the Universe; it is the power on which all things depend; it is the light by which all of life is guided. Honor the highest within yourself; for it, too, is the power on which all things depend, and the light by which all life is guided.

Dig within. Within is the well-spring of Good; and it is always ready to bubble up, if you just dig.

Marcus Aurelius ❧

You have seen a hand, a foot, or perhaps a head severed from its body and lying some distance away. Such is the state a man brings himself to—as far as he is able—when he refuses to accept what befalls him, breaks away from helping others, or when he pursues self-seeking action. He becomes an outcast from the unity of Nature; though born of it, his own hand has cut him from it. Yet here is the beautiful proviso: it lies within everyone's power to join Nature once again. God has not granted such favor to any other part of creation: once you have been separated, once you have been cleft asunder, He will, at any moment, allow you to return.

O Universe, all that is in tune with you is also in tune with me! Every note of your harmony resonates in my innermost being. For me, nothing is early and nothing is late if it is timely for you. O Nature, all that your seasons bring is fruit for me. From thee comes all things; in thee do all things live and grow; and to thee do all things return. "Dear City of God" is our cry, even though the poets say, "Dear City of the King."

Waste no more time talking about great souls and how they should be. Be one yourself!

Epictetus ⋙
SHOW ME A MAN OF GOD

Show me a Man of God.
Show me a man modeled after the doctrines
    that are ever upon his lips.
Show me a man who is hard-pressed—and happy,
In danger—and happy,
On his death-bed—and happy,
In exile—and happy,
In evil report—and happy.

Show him to me.
I ask again.

So help me, Heaven,
    I long to see *one* Man of God!
And if you cannot show me one fully realized,
    let me see one in whom the process is at work—
    or one whose bent is in that direction.
Do me that favor!
Grudge it not to an old man,
    to behold such wonder.
Do you think I wish to see the *Zeus* or *Athena* of Phidias,
    sparkling with ivory and gold?—
No. Show me one of you,
    a human soul,
        longing to be of one with God.

Epictetus ⫸

The Philosophers say that there is a God, and that His Will directs the Universe . . . But the more important lesson is to discover God's nature. Upon discovering that nature, a man would please God by making his own nature like unto God's. If the Divine is faithful, he must also be faithful; if free, he must also be free; if beneficent, he must also be beneficent; if magnanimous, he must also be magnanimous. Thus to make God's nature one's own, a man must imitate Him in every thought, word, and deed.

Epictetus ≫
A HYMN TO GOD

If we had understanding,
Would we ever cease chanting and blessing
 the Divine Power,
  both openly and in secret?
Whether digging or ploughing or eating,
 should we not sing a hymn to God?

Great is God,
 for He has given us the instruments
 to till the ground . . .
He has given us hands,
 the power of digestion,
 and the wisdom of the body that controls the breath.

Great is God,
 for He has given us a mind
 to apprehend these things
 and to duly use them!

I am old and lame—what else can I do
 but sing to God?
Were I nightingale,
 I should do after the manner of a nightingale.
Were I a swan,
 I should do after the manner of a swan.
But now, since I am a reasonable man,
 I must sing to God: this is my work.
I will do it;
 I will not desert my post . . .

And I call upon you to join this self-same hymn.

Seneca ⇛

To see a man fearless in danger,
Untainted by lust,
Happy in adversity,
Composed in turmoil,
And laughing at all those things
    which are coveted or feared by others—
All men must acknowledge,
    that this can be nothing else but a beam of divinity
    animating a human body.

Seneca

GOD IN ALL THINGS

What is God?—
>The Mind of the universe.
What is He?—
>All that you see, and all that you don't see.

Guide and guardian of the universe,
Soul and spirit of the world,
Builder and master of so great a work—
>to Him all names belong.
Would you call Him *Destiny*?
>You will not err.
Cause of causes, all things depend on Him.
Would you rather say *Providence*?
>This will be right.
By His plan the world is guided safely through its motions.
Or *Nature*?
>This title does Him no wrong.
Of Him are all things born, and in Him all things live.
Or *Universe*?
>You are not mistaken.
He is all that we see,
>wholly present in every part,
>sustaining this entire creation.

Seneca ⫸
HATRED AND LOVE

Hatred is not only a vice,
    but a vice which goes point-blank against Nature.
Hatred divides instead of joining
    and frustrates God's will in human society.
One man is born to help another.
Hatred makes us destroy one another.
Love unites—hatred separates.
Love is beneficial—hatred is destructive.
Love succors even strangers,
    hatred destroys the most intimate friendship.
Love fills all hearts with joy,
    hatred ruins all those who possess it.
Nature is bountiful, hatred is pernicious.
It is not hatred, but mutual love,
    that holds all mankind together.

The Sufi Poets

SUFISM IS THE MYSTICAL SECT OF ISLAM BASED ON love, devotion, and the soul's longing to merge with God (the Beloved). Islam means "submission," and in this regard the practice of Sufism is at the heart of Islam: although the Sufis do not attribute the same value to the traditional Muslim practices and rituals, they have submitted themselves with complete abandon to the call of Divine Love.

When Sufism first emerged in the ninth century, there were no words or poetic forms which could adequately convey the vast wealth of the Sufis' inner experience. In order to give form to their inner state, the Sufis began to create a whole new language by infusing the simple objects of this world with a new spiritual meaning. Everything around them became a mystical symbol pointing toward the path of love. The longing for God was expressed with the images of human love—the seeker taking the form of the "lover" and God becoming "the Beloved." Their divine intoxication found an expression through the images associated with worldly intoxication, such as taverns, wine, and drunkenness. These are perhaps the most humorous, and most often misinterpreted, symbols: many people who read Sufi poetry still take the words literally, thinking the Sufis are talking about actual wine. In this symbolic language of the Sufis, "wine" is the love that intoxicates the soul; "getting drunk" is losing oneself in Divine Love; the "cup" refers to one's body or heart which gets filled with "wine." They even have a word for "hangover," which denotes the lingering effects of mystical love.

Apart from the bacchanalian images, the Sufis were fond of finding ways to convey the awakening of their soul, and the journey from the corporeal to the spiritual. This notion was often expressed through the colorful images of nature and the bursting forth of spring. Using the images of love, the final union with God was termed the "wedding night"; using the images of nature, this union with the Beloved was seen as a drop of water merging into the sea. The Sufis view the state where the individual soul is separate from God as a state of misery. In Sufi poetry this separation is often portrayed as a forlorn maiden pining for her beloved; or as a helpless bird searching for its nest. Sometimes this separation is portrayed as a fish on dry land, longing for the waters of the ocean; an elephant yearning for the jungles of its native land; or even a backgammon chip striving to return to its home position. Perhaps the most vivid symbol used to depict this state of separation is the Sufi portrayed as the reed flute (*ney*) which wails aloud, longing for the reed bed from which it was cut.

The Sufi saint ***Jalaluddin Rumi*** (1207–1273) is considered "the supreme genius of Islamic mysticism," and has been called "the greatest mystical poet of any age." As a young boy he showed all the signs of saintliness and his father called him *Maulana*, "Our Master." By age twenty-four he was an acknowledged Master of Arabic grammar, Islamic law, Koranic commentary, astronomy, and Sufi lore. But it wasn't until he met his Master, Shams-i Tabriz, at the age of thirty-seven, that he came to experience the highest truth.

Many legends surround this meeting, and they all tell of the dramatic destruction of Rumi's books by Shams, and Rumi's recognition that book-knowledge could not lead him to the highest truth. Rumi's son wrote: "After meeting Shams, my father danced all day and sang all night. He had been a scholar—he became a poet; he had been an ascetic—he became drunk with love." But the ecstatic unity with his Master soon ended. Two years after meeting Shams—whom Rumi described as "the Beloved clothed in human form"—his Master suddenly disappeared, and was never seen again. Rumi was left with an unspeakable emptiness, and a grief that he tried to fill with singing and dancing. It was at this time of longing that an endless cascade of poetry began to pour from Rumi's lips. Thousands of verses flowed out as he called and called to his lost Beloved. In the end, Rumi found that he was calling to himself, that the Beloved he longed for was with him all the time. In one of his quatrains Rumi writes: "All my talk was madness, filled with *dos* and *don'ts*. For ages I knocked on a door—when it opened I found that I was knocking from the inside!"

Shamsuddin Mohammed Hafez (d. 1389) is the most famous Sufi poet among Persian-speaking people, and portions of his lyrical verses are often quoted as proverbs. Shamsuddin Mohammed Hafez, or Hafez, often used the symbolism of wine and "maidens" to describe his mystical experience, but he also lauded the great human qualities, such as love, tolerance, and generosity. Hafez lived in Shiraz (a city in Northern Iran) most of his life, and he uses the beautiful images of this city as a backdrop for many of his verses. Although Hafez scorned tradition and refused the invitations of princes, he was erudite in Arabic and Persian literature, and the name *Hafez* means "one who has memorized the Koran."

Ibn al Arabi (1165–1240) was a Muslim born in Murcia, Spain, and had a profound influence on the whole of Islamic thought. Though not Persian, his *Meccan Revelations*, and many other writings, established him as among the greatest mystics of Islam. In particular, it was his philosophy of *Unity* which influenced the whole of Islamic thinking. It says that there is no real difference between the Essence and its attributes, or, put another way, between God and the universe.

Fakhruddin Araqi (1213–1289) was a distinguished Master who, in fits of ecstasy, would reel off line upon line of inspired verse to his disciples. His poetic masterpiece, *Lama'at (Divine Flashes)*, captures the essence of Sufi thought.

Two Persian poets of lasting influence were **Abdurrahman Jami** (1414–1492) and **Mahmud Shabistari** (?1250–?1320). Jami was famed not only for his love of seclusion—spending eighteen years alone in the mountains—but also for his sheer brilliance. He was a court poet and so his work is more formal in nature than that of other Sufi poets. Shabistari's only work, *Gulshan i Raz (The Garden of Secrets)*, is revered by all as a masterpiece of Sufi literature.

Ghalib (1797–1869) was a leading mystic of Rumi's school in Istanbul, and famed for his Urdu poetry. He used the pen name "Asad." **Nazir** (1735–1846) was a singing minstrel who filled the back streets of Delhi with the sound of his guitar and the sweet longing of his voice. He was humble and simple, and regarded as the great poet of the poor. One of the earliest known Sufi works is by **Baba Kuhi of Shiraz** (d. 1050), a dervish from the famed city of Shiraz.

Rumi ≫

Come, come, whoever you are,
wanderer, worshiper, lover of leaving,
   it doesn't matter—
Ours is not a caravan of despair,
   but one of endless joy.
Even if you have broken your vows a hundred times—
Come, come, yet again, come!

Rumi ⋙

The Lover is ever drunk with love;
    He is free,
    He is mad,
He dances with ecstasy and delight.
Caught by our own thoughts,
    we worry about every little thing,
But once we get drunk on that love,
Whatever will be, will be.

When *you* dance,
    the whole universe dances.
What wonder!
I've looked,
    and now I cannot look away.
Take me, or do not take me,
    both are the same—
As long as there is life in this body,
    I am your servant.

Love came and it made me empty.
Love came and it filled me with the Beloved.
    It became the blood in my body,
    It became my arms and my legs.
    It became everything!
Now all I have is a name,
    the rest belongs to the Beloved.

Rumi

I see His face,
I see His smile,
    There is my joy!
I feel His anger,
I feel His heavy hand.
    There is my joy!
But what's this?—
    He has asked for my head!
My head doesn't matter—
He has asked me for something,
    There is my joy!

My eyes see only the face of the Beloved.
What a glorious sight,
    for that sight is beloved.
Why speak of two?—
The Beloved is in the sight,
    and the sight is in the Beloved.

There is a force within that gives you life—
    Seek that.
In your body there lies a priceless jewel—
    Seek that.
O wandering Sufi,
    if you are in search of the greatest treasure,
    don't look outside,
Look inside, and seek That.

Rumi

Our drunkenness does not comes from wine,
Our gathering, so full of cheer,
   does not come from song or dance.
Without a maiden to fill our cup,
Without friend, without music, without wine,
We burst out like madmen,
   rolling drunk on the floor.

Don't think.
Don't get lost in your thoughts.
Your thoughts are a veil on the face of the Moon.
That Moon is your heart,
   and those thoughts cover your heart.
So let them go,
   just let them fall into the water.

If you want great wealth,
   and that which lasts forever,
Don't sleep.
If you want to shine
   with the love of the Beloved,
Don't sleep.
You have slept a hundred nights,
   And what has it brought you?
For your Self, for your God,
Stay awake till dawn,
Don't sleep.

Rumi

What a day today—
There are two Suns rising.
What a day—
Not like any other day.
Look! The Light is shining in your heart!
The wheel of life has stopped.
Oh you who can see into your own heart,
What a day—
This is your day.

I cried, and I burned in that cry.
I kept silent, and I burned in that silence.
Then I stayed away from extremes—
    I went right down the middle,
And I burned in that middle.

It is said,
    "God's Light shines in all six directions."
A shout came from the crowd:
    "So where is that Light?"
    "Shall I fix my gaze to the left,
    or to the right?"
It is said,
    "For a moment, fix it neither to the left
    nor to the right."

Rumi ≫

I know nothing of two worlds,
    all I know is the One.
I seek only One,
I know only One,
I find only One,
    and I sing of only One.
I am so drunk with the wine of the Beloved
    that both worlds have slipped from my reach.
Now I have no business here,
    Save to reach for the cup of my Beloved.

Oh, I'm alive,
But this pain is worse than death.
My heart pounds, my body shakes,
    my stomach burns with pangs of hunger.
At least with hunger
    the more you eat, the better it gets,
But not with this—
    for the more I eat, the worse it gets.

O my soul,
I searched the whole world,
    but could not find you anywhere.
All I found was my Beloved.
Call me cruel,
Call me blind,
Call me anything, I don't mind,
O my soul,
    I call you *my Beloved.*

Rumi

The smile on your face is sight enough.
The sound of your Name is song enough.
Why cut me down with your deadly arrows,
   When the shadow of your whip is reason enough?

O my Beloved!
Take me,
Liberate my soul,
Fill me with your love,
   and release me from both worlds.
When I set my heart on anything but you
   a fire burns me from inside.
O my Beloved!
Take away what I want,
Take away what I do,
Take away everything
   that takes me from you.

In one sweet moment she burst from my heart.
And there she sat before me
   drinking ruby-red wine.
Trapped by her beauty I saw and I touched—
My whole face became eyes,
My every eye became hands.

Rumi ⚶

All through time that same Beauty
   has risen in a different shape,
   beckoned the soul, and disappeared.
Every moment that Loved One
   puts on a new garment—
   now of old, now of new.
Entering the heart of the world,
   like potter's clay,
   the Spirit plunged, like a diver—
Now He rises up from the mud,
   molded and baked.

He appeared as Noah and safely entered the Ark
   when a deluge flooded the world.
He became Abraham
   and walked through the midst of fire
   which turned into roses for His sake.
For a while He roamed the earth, unknown,
   helping those in need.
Then He became Jesus
   and ascended to the dome of heaven
   in glory of God.
In all, it was He
   who came and went in every generation.
Then He appeared in the form of the Prophet
   and gained the empire of Islam.

   What essence is preserved?
   What moves from one reality to the next?

The lovely Winner of Hearts became a sword
   and appeared in the hand of Ali,
   the slayer of time.

When Mansur yelled out, "I am the Truth,"
    they hanged him as a heretic.
But no! It was *He* who cried out,
    "I am the Truth."
It was *He* who mounted the scaffold.

Rumi has spoken the truth.
But no! Do not listen to Rumi—
    It is *He* who speaks the truth.

Rumi ⋙

On that final day
When my casket moves along
Do not think my soul
    will stay in this world.

Do not weep for me, crying, *Tragedy, tragedy.*
You will only fall into the snares of delusion—
    Now that's a tragedy!

When you see my lifeless body go by
Do not cry out, *Gone, gone.*
It is my moment of union.
It is when I come upon
    the eternal embrace of my Beloved.

As I am lowered into the ground
Do not say, *Farewell, farewell.*
For the grave is but a veil
    covering the splendor of Paradise.

    Having seen the fall
    Consider the rise.
    What harm ever came to the setting Sun or Moon?

What appears to you as a setting
    is for me a rising.
What appears to you as a prison
    is for my soul an endless garden.

Every seed that enters the earth will grow.
Should it be any different with a human seed?
Every bucket that is lowered into a well comes up full.

Should I complain when instead of water
   I pull up Joseph himself?

Do not look for your words here,
   look for them over there.
Sing to me in the silence of your heart
   and I will rise up
     to hear your triumphant song.

Rumi ⋙

Be off and know
That the way of lovers is opposite all other ways.
Lies from the Friend
Are better than truth and kindness from others.

For Him the impossible is commonplace,
Punishment is reward,
Tyranny is justice,
Slander is high praise.

His harshness is soft,
His blasphemy is sacred.
The blood that drips from the Beloved's thorn
    is sweeter than roses and basil.

When He's bitter
    it's better than a candy shop.
When He turns His head away
    it's all hugs and kisses.
When He says, "By God, I've had enough of you!"
    it's like an eternal spring
    flowing from the fountain of life.

A "No" from His lips is a thousand times "Yes."
On this selfless path
    He acts like a stranger
    yet He's your dearest friend.

His infidelity is faith,
His stones are jewels,
His holding back is giving,
His ruthlessness is mercy.

You may laugh at me and say,
    "The path you're on is full of curves!"
Yes—for the curve of his eyebrow
    I have traded in my soul!

This curvy path has gotten me drunk,
I cannot say another word!
Carry on my glorious heart,
    finish the poem in silence . . .

    O Shams, Lord of Tabriz,
    What sweetness you pour upon me—
    All I need do is open my mouth
            and all your songs flow out.

Rumi ≫

Last night I learned how to be a lover of God
To live in this world and call nothing my own.

I looked inward
And the beauty of my own emptiness
   filled me till dawn.
It enveloped me like a mine of rubies.
Its hue clothed me in red silk.

Within the cavern of my soul
I heard the voices of lovers crying,
"Drink now! Drink now!"—

I took a sip and saw the vast ocean—
Wave upon wave caressed my soul.
The lovers of God dance around
And the circle of their steps
   becomes a ring of fire round my neck.

Heaven calls me with its rain and thunder—
a hundred thousand cries
yet I cannot hear . . .

   All I hear is the call of my Beloved.

Rumi ⟫

This is love—to fly upward
    toward the endless heavens.
To rend a hundred veils at every moment.
At the first breath, to give up life;
At the final step, to go without feet.
To see the world as a dream
    and not as it appears.

O heart, what a blessing it is
To join the circle of lovers,
    To see beyond sight,
    To know the secrets within every breast.

O soul, from where comes your life
And the power of your spirit?
    Tell me, speak in the language of birds,
    And I will understand.

My soul said:
They brought me to God's workshop,
Where all things take form, and I flew.
Before this form of mine
    even took shape—I flew and I flew.
And when I could fly no longer
They dragged me into this form,
    and locked me into this house
    of water and clay.

Now I am here—
    What else can I do but love?

Rumi ⅍

Happy is the moment, when we sit together,
With two forms, two faces, yet one soul,
　　you and I.

The flowers will bloom forever,
The birds will sing their eternal song,
The moment we enter the garden,
　　you and I.

The stars of heaven will come out to watch us,
And we will show them
　　the light of a full moon,
　　you and I.

No thoughts of "you," no thoughts of "I,"
Just the bliss of union—
Joyous, alive, free of care,
　　you and I.

All the bright-winged birds of heaven
Will swoop down to drink our sweet water—
The ocean of our laughter,
　　you and I.

What a miracle of fate, us sitting here.
Even at the far ends of the earth
We would still be together,
　　you and I.

We have one form in this world,
　　another in the next.
To us belongs an eternal heaven,
　　the endless delight,
　　you and I.

Hafez
THE PROPHET

The dark and beautiful one—
    the sweetness of the world is with him.
His charming eye and laughing lip—
    the joy of all hearts is with him.

The prophets are the greatest among men,
But he is the Sultan of the age—
    the seal of God is with him.

A black mark adorns his golden face.
For a grain of wheat
    Adam was turned out of paradise.
Why?—the reason why is with him.

O friends, the Heart-Ravisher is gone.
In God's Name, what will I do with my wounded heart—
    the healing ointment is with him.

His face is fair, his skill perfect, his dress pure.
In all its glory, the Pure One is with him.

Who will understand this paradox?—
The stone-hearted Beloved slew us
    yet the life-giving breath is with him.

Hafez is one of true faith—hold him dear:
For the salvation of many great souls is with him.

Hafez

THE CUP OF KING JAMSHID

For years my heart sought the Cup of Jamshid,
Seeking from others what it already had.

From men wandering aimlessly by the sea,
I asked about the pearl beyond the shell of time and place.

Last night I took my problems to a Magian priest;
I heard he could unsnare my soul with but one glance.
I found him smiling, joyous, a cup of wine in his hand.
He was gazing into a mirror that revealed a hundred sights.
I said, "When did the Wise One give you that cup?"
He said, "On the day He created the azure vault of heaven."
He said: "The gallows raised its head for Hallaj;
His crime was telling the truth to those who could not under-
    stand."
"If the grace of the holy spirit offers its help again,
Others, too, would raise the dead like Jesus."

I asked: "When will I escape from the snares of the Beloved?"
He said, "Hafez is complaining about the length of his wedding
    night!"

Hafez
DO NOT FALL INTO SADNESS

Joseph is lost, he'll find his way back to Canaan—
 do not fall into sadness.
One day your dreary cell will turn into a rose garden—
 do not fall into sadness.

O heart torn by sorrow, become your joyous self again,
Don't show us tears,
Come back to your senses! What's in your head?—
 do not fall into sadness.

The Spring is in bloom; make your throne in the garden!
O songbird under a canopy of roses—
 do not fall into sadness.

Though the door of secrets has not yet opened,
 don't give up hope;
Within your sight lies the secret of every soul—
 do not fall into sadness.

Who in this world ever grieved
 without gaining the compassion of a Master?
Suffering brings the one who removes all suffering—
 do not fall into sadness.

At your command, the heavens would stop for two days.
Even the circling spheres would change their course for you—
 do not fall into sadness

Your feet are scorched by the desert sand,
Your skin is scarred by the Arabian thorns,
Carry on, you will soon reach the Ka'be—
 do not fall into sadness.

O heart, a raging flood has swept away your home,
But Noah himself has come to steer your boat—
    do not fall into sadness.

The play of life is tragic,
    and the plot remains unknown,
Yet there is no road without an end—
    do not fall into sadness

In the corner, on a lonely night,
    you pray and read the holy book.
O Hafez, one day the Beloved will be yours—
    do not fall into sadness.

Hafez

DO NOT ASK

What pain I have endured on the path of love?—do not ask.
What is the taste of love's poison?—do not ask.

I have wandered throughout the world, and in the end
I choose the Heart-Ravishing Beloved. Why?—do not ask.

When I reached the dust of His feet;
Why did my tears run over?—do not ask.

What words did He
Whisper in my ear last night?—do not ask.

He put His finger on my lips and said, "Don't speak."
How sweet was the kiss of those ruby lips?—do not ask.

Sitting alone, in the darkness of my own greed,
What sorrows have I endured?—do not ask.

Hafez has taken one step on the path of love,
Oh what heights he has attained?—do not ask.

Hafez ⇾

By the sparkle of your eye, O bestower of grace;
By the folds of your hair,
   O singer of joyous songs;

By the sweetness of your ruby lips,
   O fountain of life;
By the scent of your perfume,
   O springtime of beauty;

By the dust of your path—
   the sparkling lights of heaven;
By the dust of your feet—
   the envy of pure water;

By your moon-like splendor,
By the rising Sun,
By your heavenly threshold,
By the majestic sky,

By your sweet compassion,
By your breath of roses,
By the fragrance of your tresses,
By the scent of the Northerly breeze,

By your ruby lips—
   the jewel of the lover's hopeful eye;
By the shining pearl of your words—
   the treasury of all eloquence;

By the smooth touch of your cheek—
   the rose-petals of my sight;

By your endless eyes—
    the garden wherein I could roam forever—

I swear that if Hafez finds joy in anyone but you
He'll give up his life in this world.

Hafez

One word from the song of our union, and I will rise.
Like the bird of paradise, from the snares of this world I will rise.

By my love I swear, if you call on me to be your servant
I will renounce the rulership of both worlds, and rise.

O Lord, let the water of life fall from your guiding cloud.
From the midst of a handful of dust, I will rise.

Sit at the head of my tomb with a cup of wine and a happy song.
From your fragrance and your joyful dancing, I will rise.

Though I am old, hold me in your arms for one night.
When morning comes, all my youth will rise.

O Dancer of Beauty, stand up and show us your radiant form.
For one glimpse, Hafez will bid farewell to this world, and rise.

Hafez

O Breeze, you have the Beloved's fragrance,
You have the smell of his musky perfume.

Beware! Do not reach out to touch his hair—
What business do you have with those curls?

O Rose! How can you compare to his lovely face?—
He has exquisite fragrance, you have a load of thorns.

O Sweet Basil! How can you compare to the smell of his hair?—
He has the sky, you have the dust.

O Narcissus! How can you compare to his ravishing eye?—
He is filled with bliss, you have a hangover.

O Cypress! How can you compare to his lofty stature?—
He is in the garden, you are among the weeds.

O Reason! How can you compare to his boundless love?
He holds the world in his hand; all you have is a handful.

Hafez, one day you will join the Beloved
But only if you have the strength to wait.

Ibn al Arabi ⁂

O dear one, listen!
I am the reality of the world, the center of the circle.
I am the parts and the whole.
I am the will holding Heaven and Earth in place.
I have given you sight only so you may see me.

O dear one!
I call again and again but you do not hear me,
I appear again and again but you do not see me,
I fill myself with fragrance, again and again,
    but you do not smell me.
I become savory food yet you do not taste me.
Why can't you reach me through your touch
Or breathe me in through your sweet perfumes?

Love me,
Love yourself in me.
No one is deeper within you than I.
Others may love you for their own sake,
But I love you for yourself.

Dear one!
This bargain is not fair—
If you take one step toward me,
It is only because I have taken a hundred toward you.
I am closer to you than yourself.
Closer than your soul, than your own breath.
Why do you not see me?
Why do you not hear me?
    I am so jealous—
I want you to see me—and no one else.
To hear me—and no one else,
    not even yourself.

Dear one! Come with me.
Let us go to Paradise together.
And if we find any road
    that leads to separation,
We will destroy that road.
Let us go hand in hand
In the presence of Love.
Let it be our witness,
Let it forever seal
    this wondrous union of ours.

Araqi

I look into the mirror and see my own beauty;
I see the Truth of the universe revealing itself as me.
I rise in the sky as the morning Sun. Do not be surprised—
Every particle of creation is my own form.

What are the holy spirits?—My essence revealed.
And the human body?—The vessel of my own form.
What is the ocean that encircles the world?—
    A drop of my abundant Grace;
And the purest light that fills every soul?—
    A spark of my own illumination.

What is the water that grants eternal life?—
    A drop of my divine nectar.
And the breath that brings the dead back to life?—
    A puff of my breath, the breath of all life.

I am Light itself, reflected in the heart of everyone.
I am the treasure of the Divine Name,
    the shining Essence of all things.

From the highest heavens to the bedrock of the earth
All is but a shadow of my splendor.

If I dropped the veil covering my true essence
The world would be lost in a flash of brilliant light.

Araqi ⫸

Love courses through everything,
No, Love *is* everything.
How can you say *there is no love*
    when nothing but Love exists?
All that you see has appeared because of Love.
    All shines from Love,
    All pulses with Love,
    All flows from Love—
No, once again, all *is* Love!

His Light rose,
    I found it in my own heart—
It is now my Light
    you see shining!

Araqi

This world is nothing but a dance of shadows,
A line drawn between
    darkness and light,
    joy and oppression,
    time and eternity.
Learn to read this subtle line
    for it tells all the secrets of creation.

Let go of everything,
Completely lose yourself on this path,
Then you will have no doubts.
With absolute conviction you'll cry out—
I am God!
I am the one I have found!

In the light I praised you
    and never knew it.
In the dark I stayed with you
    and never knew it.
I always thought that I was me,
But no—I was you
    and never knew it.

Jami

All through eternity
    God unveils His exquisite form.
In the solitude of nothingness
He holds a mirror to His own Face
    and beholds His own beauty.
He is the knower and the known,
    the seer and the seen;
No eye but His own
    has ever looked upon this Universe.

His every quality
    finds a form and an expression:
Eternity becomes the verdant fields of Time and Space.
Love becomes the life-giving garden of this world.
Every branch and leaf and fruit
Reveals some aspect of His perfection—
    The cypress gives hint of His majesty,
    The rose gives tidings of His beauty.

Wherever God looks,
    Love is always there;
Wherever God shows a rosy cheek,
    Love lights Her fire from that flame.
Whenever God dwells in the dark folds of night,
    Love comes and finds a heart
    entangled in the tresses.
God and Love are as body and soul.
God is the mine, Love is the diamond.

They have been together
    since the beginning . . .
    in every beat of every heart.

shabistari ≫

"I" and "you" are Pure Radiance,
Beams of one Light
  shining through the niches of a lamp.
Lift yourself above time and space
  and become time and space.
Leave behind this world
  and became a world unto yourself.

When "I" and "you" are bound by form,
  a veil falls between us and our love.
Lift the veil
  and you will see all people as one.
Lift the veil and you will ask:
    What is a mosque?
    What is a synagogue?
    What is a fire-temple?

shabistari ⚛

The eye is not strong enough
    to look at the brilliant sun,
But you can watch its light
    reflected in water.
Pure Being is too bright to behold,
    yet it can be seen
    reflected in the mirror of this world . . .

Every particle of the world is a mirror.
In each atom lies the light
    of a thousand suns.
Cleave the heart of a raindrop
    and a hundred pure oceans will flow forth.
Look closely at a grain of sand
    and the seed of a thousand beings can be seen.
The foot of an ant is larger than an elephant.
In essence, a drop of water
    does not differ from the Nile.
In the heart of a barley-corn
    lies the bounty of a hundred harvests.
Within the pulp of a millet seed
    an entire universe can be found.
In the wing of a fly,
    an ocean of wonder.
In the pupil of the eye, an endless heaven.
Though the chamber of the heart is small,
    it's large enough for the Lord of both worlds
    to gladly make His home there.

shabistari

The tavern-haunter is a seeker of Unity,
    a soul freed from the shackles
    of himself.

The tavern is where lovers meet,
    the place where the bird of the soul takes rest.
It is a sanctuary that does not exist
    in a world that cannot be found.
The tavern-haunter wanders alone
    in a desolate place,
    seeing the whole world as a mirage.
The desert he walks through
    has no limit;
No one can reach its end.
You may wander there for a hundred years
    and never see yourself or another.
Those who live there
    possess neither head nor feet,
    neither faith nor infidelity.
Drinking the wine of dispassion
    they have renounced good and evil.
Sipping from a cup of bliss,
    without lips or mouth,
They have cast away
All thoughts of name and fame,
All talk of marvels and visions,
All dreams of secret chambers and distant worlds.

They fall, and they rise again,
    between union and separation.
Now shedding tears of blood;
Now rising up to a world of bliss,
    stretching out their necks like racers.

Now with blackened faces staring at a wall,
Or faces reddened by the wine of Unity.
Now in a mystic whirl,
    dancing in the arms of their Beloved,
      losing head and foot like the turning heavens.
With every strain the minstrel plays,
    the rapture of the unseen world unfolds;
With every note of this mystic song
    a veil is torn from a priceless treasure.

They are blind to this world,
Indifferent to great and small,
Ignorant of Master and disciple.

They guzzle down cup after cup of wine
    and still they want more!
They sweep ancient dust from their souls.
They grab at the Beloved's dress
    like a bunch of drunkards!

So who are these guys?—
They are Sufis.

Ghalib

I leave with scars
    and the ache of longings still unmet.
I am a candle,
    blown naked by the wind—
    not fit to stand at the table
    where men rejoice.

Everyone! Come!
Our door is open, our vision is clear.
Here we see only what is true—
"The high, the low, the good, the bad"—
    we see none of this.

My yearning has loosened
    the veil hiding Beauty.
She is now mine—but alas,
My own sight
    is blocking the view.

The beat of my own heart
    is sounding.
The wish to live as others do
    has long been gone.
What does their world have to offer?—
Nothing by the echo of voices
    yelling, "More, more."

"I do not fear love's cruelty."
But Asad, your heart,
    which beats so proudly,
    is the first thing She will take.

Ghalib

This world is nothing more than
　　Beauty's chance to show Herself.
And what are we?—
Nothing more than Beauty's chance to see Herself.
For if Beauty were not seeking Herself,
　　we would not exist.

Every particle of creation
　　sings its own song
　　of what is, and of what is not.
The wise hear what is;
The mad hear what is not—
And only a cracked mirror
　　will show a difference.

All your knowledge
　　leads you in the wrong direction.
All your worship
　　only puts you to sleep.
Insipid is this world
　　which only believes in what is seen;
Here, taste the wine from a Cup
　　that cannot be seen.

The one who has adorned himself
　　with the Creator's form
Is the only one fit to guard
　　the purity of both worlds.

On account of those who repeat His Name,
This Earth has become a paradise,
　　an honored place
　　in the order of creation.
God's love is on this Earth,
And the heavens
　　forever bend over to greet Her.

Nazir

My dear friend,
How am I to tell of the many vagaries
    on the path of love?
How am I to speak of what happened to me?

One day, suddenly,
    tears began to flow from my eyes
And I was filled with the desire
    to find the one
    whom everyone adores.

All poise and decorum left me
    and a yearning to meet the Beloved
    rose within my heart.
I became impatient, restless,
    unmindful of my actions.

I dyed my garments in red
    and put a garland around my neck.
I rubbed ashes on my body,
    adorned myself with a string of beads,
    and renounced the world.
Thus attired, I began my quest.

As a renunciant
    I looked for my Beloved
    from door to door.
In the lanes and in the streets
I searched for Him.

My heart was burning with fire.
Sometimes I howled like a madman,
Other times I cried like a baby.
Sighs from my lips came out as hot vapor;

A flood of tears fell from my eyes,
    and all the world spun round me.
My madness drew a crowd.
I sought my Friend in flesh and blood
    but all I ever got were excuses.

Whoever came before me I asked,
    "Where can I meet my Beloved?"

Sometimes I took to a rosary.
With every bead that passed through my fingers I asked,
    "Where is He? Where is He?"

I knew nothing.
I did not know what to seek,
I did not know where to go.
Whom was I to ask, where was I to wander?
What path to follow?
What instructions to pursue
    whereby I might find my Beloved?

Seeking Him I reached the mosque,
But all I found were vain discussions
    on sacraments and ceremonials.

My heart told me to go to a seminary;
Maybe there I might meet my Lord.
But all I met there were noisy debates
    and scholars puffed with eloquence.

I was advised to go visit the temple.
I found nothing there but
    idols being worshiped
    and gongs being sounded.
Disgusted, I sought a stone
    to strike against my head.

For nowhere could I find
    that callous Beloved of mine.

Then I went on a pilgrimage
    to all the holy sights.
Maybe I would find Him there.
So I stopped at many holy places
    and bowed before many deities,
But it brought me no comfort.
And when I found myself helpless
    I left the towns and its temples
    to wander in the jungle.

In the wilderness I wept and shed hot tears.
I asked myself, "How long must I bear this agony
    of separation?"
But there was nowhere to go,
    no place to find shelter from my pain.

For days I roamed in the forest—
    a poor man, a pilgrim, a homeless *fakir.*
In the mountains too, I struggled.
I was empty, hungry, thirsty—in a miserable plight,
    without a morsel to appease my hunger,
    without a drop to quench my thirst.

I laid myself out in a field,
    the burning sun was overhead.
My mind filled with the desire to see Him
But all was in vain—
The Lord would not
    show Himself to me.
I shed tears of blood
    that sparkled like rubies in the sands.

When I reached a state of total despair,
   hoping that death
   might rescue me from this pain,
   He, my careless Beloved,
Came to me.
Like a mother rushing to her sick child,
He came to me,
   sat by my side,
   and placed my head upon His lap.
Kind words came from His lips:

"Now see whatever you want to see,
I will reveal to you all the secrets of my heart.
Remember, first We test our lover.
We torment him, oppress him,
   and force him to shed tears.
Then We bring him to us.
When all his thoughts are of the Beloved,
We allow him to come near,
   shower him with grace,
   and hold him in our arms.
Thus he becomes perfect."

As these words reached my ears
I came back to life, gained consciousness,
   and was free of all pain.
Then I cast one look
   at His radiant face
And the mystery of all creation
   lay bare before me.
In one moment
   the good and bad actions of lifetimes
   vanished.

From separation I passed into Unity;
All the illusions of life disappeared
   like a phantom show.

Now, wherever I cast my glance,
I see Him and none other.
The Muslim, the Hindu, and the Jew
Have all become the same to me—
    they have all merged in the
Glory of my one Beloved.

So says Nazir.

Baba Kuhi of Shiraz

ONLY GOD I SAW

In the market, in the cloister—only God I saw.
In the valley and on the mountain—only God I saw.
Him I have seen beside me oft in tribulation;
In favour and in fortune—only God I saw.
In prayer and in fasting, in praise and contemplation,
In the religion of the Prophet—only God I saw.
Neither soul nor body, accident nor substance,
Qualities nor causes—only God I saw.
I opened mine eyes and by the light of His face around me
In all the eye discovered—only God I saw.
Like a candle I was melting in his fire;
Amidst the flames outflashing—only God I saw.
Myself with mine own eyes I saw most clearly,
But when I looked with God's eyes—only God I saw.
I passed away into nothingness, I vanished,
And lo, I was the All-living—only God I saw.

The Christian Saints

CHRISTIANITY BEGAN AS A SECT OF JUDAISM. AT first the only difference between this sect and Judaism was its interpretation of the Messianic prophesies of the Hebrew Scriptures: traditional Judaism believed that the Messiah was yet to come; the Nazarenes (a name used for the earliest Christians) believed that he already appeared, in the form of Jesus Christ. With the increasing number of gentile converts and the acceptance of new ideas, Christianity broke from its roots and became a completely new religion of love and devotion, humility and faith, interior prayer, worship, and the adoration of Jesus Christ. The writings about Jesus and his disciples, along with the traditional Hebrew texts, became part of the written heritage of this new religion.

Christianity might have remained a small Messianic cult had it not been for the efforts of **Saint Paul** (A.D. ?3–64). As a youth, Paul was one of the Jewish authorities who fiercely suppressed this emerging sect. But the spiritual visions he had on the road to Damascus—dazzling lights, voices, sudden darkness—convinced him that he had seen and heard the risen Christ, and that Christ was the Messiah. The next thirty years of Saint Paul's life were spent traveling, teaching, writing letters, and unifying the many newly found Christian groups. Through his dynamic leadership the precepts of this new faith were shaped into a compelling and universal religion of salvation. Called "the second father of Christianity," Saint Paul is truly an epochal figure in history.

One of the earliest works on the basic practice of Christianity is the **Philokalia** (1st–4th centuries A.D.), a collection of writings by monks and abbots who applied Jesus' teachings to their own lives. One notable practice of these early monks was the ceaseless Jesus Prayer—the continuous and uninterrupted calling of the name of Jesus with lips, mind, and soul. Both the *Philokalia* and the Jesus Prayer were made famous in the West by an unknown **Russian Monk** (19th century) who, in his book *The Way of a Pilgrim*, tells of his spiritual adventures throughout Russia and the joy, happiness, and protection that comes from ceaseless prayer.

One of the most influential Christian figures of the Middle Ages was the German preacher and theologian **Meister Eckhart** (1260–1329), whose ideas and writings—though officially condemned by the Catholic Church—were embraced by the great Christian mystics. With great intellectual power and an "air of almost terrible certainty," Eckhart wrote about his own experience of becoming one with God. He writes, "There is nothing so easy to me, so possible, as to be God." And again, "The soul is not *like* God—the soul is God."

In the later part of the 14th century arose a movement called *devotio moderna*, the New Devotion, which emphasized the practice of complete surrender of selfhood and total devotion to God. This movement gave rise to the great mystic **Thomas à Kempis** (1380–1471), a monk and a recluse whose book, *The Imitation of Christ*, ranks second only to the Bible in its profound and lasting influence throughout Christendom. The New Devotion is also echoed in the writings of the French priest **Jean Pierre de Caussade** (1675–1751), who saw the essence of Christianity, and all religious practice, as pivoting on the purity of one's heart and complete surrender to the Will of God. To him every moment and every event in life was sacred because "God speaks to everyone through what is happening to them moment by moment."

Saint Paul ⟫
LOVE

Though I speak with the tongues of men and angels,
And have not love,
I am no better than a clanging gong
    or a brass bell.
And though I have the gift of prophecy,
    and know every hidden mystery;
      and though I have faith enough to move mountains,
And have not love,
    I am nothing.
And though I give away all I own to the poor,
    and offer my body to be burned,
And have not love,
    I do not gain a thing.

Love is patient, love is kind,
Love knows not jealousy,
Love is never boastful,
    nor proud, nor unseemly.
Love is not selfish nor easily provoked.
Love knows nothing of wrong
    and does not rejoice at the misfortune of others.
    It only delights in the Truth.
There is nothing love cannot bear,
    no limit to its faith, its hope, or its endurance.

The reign of love will never end.
But where there are prophesies, they will end;
Where there are tongues of ecstasy, they will end;
Where there is knowledge, it will end.
For our knowledge is only of a part,
    and our prophesies tell of but a part.
And that which is a part vanishes
    with the arrival of the whole.

When I was a child,
    I spoke as a child, I saw as a child,
    and I thought as a child.
When I grew up, I put away childish things.
Now we see everything through a murky glass,
    but one day we will see God clearly,
    face to face.
Now my knowledge is incomplete,
    one day it will be perfect,
    like God's knowledge of me.

In a word,
    never let go of these three things:
Faith, hope, and love.
And know that the greatest of these
    will always be love.

Saint Paul ⟫
THE APOSTLES

All of you, no doubt, have everything you could desire. You have come into your fortune already. You have come into your kingdom—and left us out. How I wish you had indeed won your kingdom; then you might share it with us! For it seems that God has made us apostles the most abject of mankind. We are like men condemned to death in the arena, a spectacle to the whole universe—angels as well as men. We are fools for Christ's sake, while you are so sensible Christians. We are weak; you are so powerful. We are in disgrace; you are honored. To this day we go hungry and thirsty and in rags; we are roughly handled; we wander from place to place; we wear ourselves out working with our hands. They curse us, and we bless; they persecute us, and we submit to it; they slander us, and we humbly make our appeal . . .

Honor and dishonor, praise and blame, are alike our lot; we are the impostors who speak the truth, the unknown men whom all men know; dying, we still live on; disciplined by suffering, we are not done to death; in our sorrows, we always have cause for joy; poor ourselves, we bring wealth to many; without a penny, we own the world.

Saint Paul ≫

THE SPIRIT

There are a variety of gifts, but the same Spirit. There are varieties of service, but the same Lord. There are many forms of work, but all of them, in all men, are the work of the same God. In each of us the Spirit is manifested in one particular way, for some useful purpose. One man, through the Spirit, has the gift of wise speech, while another, by the power of the same Spirit, can put the deepest knowledge into words. Another, by the same Spirit, is granted faith; another, by the one Spirit, gifts of healing, and another miraculous powers; another has the gift of prophecy, and another ability to distinguish true spirits from false; yet another the gift of ecstatic utterance of different kinds, and another the ability to interpret it. But all these gifts are the work of one and the same Spirit, distributing them separately to each individual at will.

Surely you know that you are God's temple, where the Spirit of God dwells. Anyone who destroys God's temple will himself be destroyed by God, because the temple of God is holy; and you are that temple.

If we were willing to make even small efforts, we would not suffer either much distress or difficulty. For if a man urges himself to make efforts, then, as he continues them, he gradually makes progress and later practices virtues with tranquillity; for God, seeing him urge himself, sends him help. So let us urge ourselves, for, although we have not reached perfection, if we make efforts, through efforts we shall receive help, and with this help shall acquire all kinds of virtues. Therefore one of the fathers said, "Give blood and receive spirit," that is, strive earnestly and you will become perfect.

A soul pure in God is God.

The wise Solomon says in the Proverbs, "They that have no guidance fall like leaves; but in much counsel there is safety." So you see what the Holy Scriptures teach us? They enjoin us not to rely on ourselves, not to regard ourselves as knowing all, not to believe that we can control ourselves, for we need help, and are in need of those who would counsel us according to God. No men are more unfortunate or nearer perdition than those who have no teachers on the way of God.

For what does it mean that where no guidance is, the people fall like leaves? A leaf is at first green, flourishing, beautiful; then it gradually withers, falls, and is finally trampled underfoot. So it is with a man who has no guide: at first he is always zealous in fasting, vigil, silence, obedience, and other virtues; then his zeal, little by little, cools down and, having no one to instruct, support, and fire him up with zeal, he insensibly withers, falls, and finally becomes a slave of the enemies, who do with him what they will.

One of perfect prayer is he who,
    withdrawing from all mankind,
    is united with all mankind.
One of perfect prayer is he who
    regards himself as existing with all people
    and sees himself in every person.

Meister Eckhart ❧
FILLING THE EMPTINESS

God must act when He finds you ready; for God cannot leave anything empty in man or in nature. Although you do not sense His presence, and feel totally empty of Him, I assure you this is not the case. For if there existed anything empty under heaven, either heaven would draw it up to itself or bend down to fill it with itself. God, the Lord of all creation, must fill all that is empty.

I maintain by God's eternal truth that God must pour Himself, without reservation, with all His powers, into everyone who has sunk completely into himself and has touched bottom. For it is God's very nature to give Himself to all those who are empty. And God will give Himself so fully and completely that nothing will be left of Himself—nothing will be left of His essence, His nature, nor His creation. God must pour everything, His totality, into that person who has completely given himself to Him.

On his way to church, a scholar was surprised to see a man in tattered clothes and barefoot. Nevertheless, as a good Christian, he greeted the poor man: "May God give you a good morning."

The poor man cheerfully replied, "I have never had a bad morning."

"Then may God give you luck."

"I have never had bad luck."

"Well, may God give you happiness."

"I have never been unhappy."

The scholar then asked the man, "Could you please explain yourself to me? I do not understand your answers."

"With pleasure!" the poor man replied. "You wish me a good morning, yet I have never had a bad morning. For when I am hungry, I praise God. When I am cold, when it is raining or snowing, I praise God. That is why I have never had a bad morning. You wish that God may give me luck. However, I have never had bad luck. This is because I live with God and always feel that what He does is for the best. Whatever God sends me, be it pleasant or unpleasant, I accept with a grateful heart. That is why I have never had bad luck. Finally, you wish that God should make me happy. But I have never been unhappy. For all I desire is to follow God's will. I have surrendered my will so totally to God, and so, whatever God wants I also want. That is why I have never been unhappy."

Meister Eckhart

A PERFECT WILL

A perfect and true will is one completely aligned with God and void of everything else. The more a man succeeds in following God's will, the more he unites himself with God. So, if someone wished to touch him, he would first have to touch God. If someone wanted to approach him, he would first have to pass through God. By aligning with God's will, a person takes on the taste of God: grief and joy, bitterness and sweetness, darkness and light— and all of life—becomes a divine gift.

I will never ask God to give Himself to me. All I ask is that He makes me pure and empty. For it is God's very nature to give Himself to those who are pure, and to fill those who are empty.

Meister Eckhart ⫸
THE SOUL IS GOD

Come now, noble souls, and take a look at the splendor you are carrying within yourselves! But if you do not let go of yourself completely, if you do not drown yourself in this bottomless sea of the Godhead, you cannot get to know this divine light.

When the soul is totally lost, it finds that it is the very self it had sought for so long in vain. Here the soul *is* God. Here it enjoys supreme bliss. Here it is sufficient unto itself. Here it shines with its own radiance. Here, at last, it has found that the Kingdom of God is itself!

There is no need to look for God here or there. He is no farther away than the door of your own heart. There He stands waiting till He finds you ready to open the door and let Him enter. No need for you to call Him from afar—He is waiting more impatiently than you for that door to open. He wants you a thousand times more urgently than you want Him. There is only one thing you must do—open the door and enter.

No one has ever longed so much for anything as God longs to bring man to Him. God is so close to us, but we are distant and turned away from Him. God is within, we are without. God is at home with us, but we are strangers to ourselves.

Meister Eckhart ⫸
DIVINE BIRTH

Never has anything become so kindred, so alike, so one with another, as the soul becomes with God in this birth . . . In this birth,
God flows into the soul with such dazzling light that God and the
soul merge into one—one spirit, one essence, one Being.

God has given birth to the Son as you, as me, as each one of us. As
many beings—as many gods in God.

In my soul, God not only gives birth to me as His son, He
gives birth to me as *Himself*, and Himself as me.

My physical father is my father with but a small part of his
being, and I live my life separate from him. He may be dead, and I
may live. God, however, is my father with His entire being, and I
am never separate from Him. I am always His; I am alive only because He is alive.

In this divine birth I find that God and I are the same: I am what I
was and what I shall remain, now and forever. I am carried above
the highest angels. I neither increase nor decrease, for in this birth
I have become the motionless cause of all that moves. I have won
back what has always been mine. Here, in my own soul, the greatest of all miracles has taken place—God has returned to God!

Meister Eckhart ⁂
GOD'S WILL

In every moment I am perfectly content with God's will and per-fectly pleased that He is making it known to me. His will is so dear and so precious that following it is far more important than any-thing God might give me. In this way, all gifts would be mine and all beings would be God. Life may present me with its best or its worst—this would neither add nor take away one speck of my joy. How then can I complain, seeing that the sum of all human gifts belongs to me? Truly, I am so content with God's care of me—with whatever He gives or does not give me—that there is not the slightest difference between what I have and the best I could ever wish for myself.

Think of Him alone and never mind whether God is doing your work or whether you are doing it yourself. If your thoughts are set on Him, whether God wills it or not, He must do your work.

Meister Eckhart ⬩

It is my humility which gives God His divinity, and here is the proof: It is God's inherent nature to give. But God cannot give if there is no one to receive His gifts. If, then, by my humility, I become receptive to what God has to give, I make God a giver. And since it has always been God's nature to give, I, by my humility, give God what is already His. A generous man who wants to be a giver must first find a taker, since without a taker he cannot be a giver . . . So, if God is to give, He must first find someone who will receive; and none but the humble can receive the gift of God. Therefore, God's divine power of giving is quite dependent upon my humility: without my humility God can give me nothing, nor can I receive anything. That is why I, by my humility, give God His divinity.

It is surely true, in all situations, that he who wholly gives up his will to God will catch God and bind him so that He can do nothing but what that man wills! Completely surrender your will to God, and in return He will give you His will, so fully and without reserve, that it will become your own. This is God's promise—He swore it to Himself—belonging to you, He can do nothing other than what you wish. But, God can never belong to anyone who has not first become His own.

The eye by which I see God is the same as the eye by which God sees me. My eye and God's eye are one and the same—one in seeing, one in knowing, and one in loving.

The Christian Saints   163

Russian Monk ⚛

By the grace of God I am a Christian man . . . and by calling a homeless wanderer of the humblest birth who roams from place to place. My worldly goods are a knapsack with some dried bread in it on my back, and in my breast pocket a Bible. And that is all.

A Christian is bound to perform many good works, but before all else what he ought to do is pray, for without prayer no other good work whatever can be accomplished. Without prayer he cannot find the way to the Lord, he cannot understand the truth, he cannot crucify the flesh with its passions and lusts, his heart cannot be enlightened with the light of Christ, he cannot be savingly united to God. None of those things can be effected unless they are preceded by constant prayer.

Russian Monk ⫸

When I prayed with my heart, everything around me seemed delightful and marvelous. The trees, the grass, the birds, the earth, the air, the light seemed to be telling me that they existed for man's sake, that they witnessed to the love of God for man, that everything proved the love of God for man, that all things prayed to God and sang His praise.

Sometimes my understanding, which had been so stupid before, was given so much light that I could easily grasp and dwell upon matters of which up to now I had not been able even to think at all. Sometimes that sense of a warm gladness in my heart spread throughout my whole being and I was deeply moved as the fact of the presence of God everywhere was brought home to me. Sometimes by calling upon the name of Jesus I was overwhelmed with bliss, and now I knew the meaning of the words *"The kingdom of God is within you."*

The prayer of my heart gave me such consolation that I felt there was no happier person on earth than I, and I doubted if there could be greater and fuller happiness in the kingdom of Heaven. Not only did I feel this in my own soul, but the whole outside world also seemed to me full of charm and delight. Everything drew me to love and thank God: people, trees, plants, animals. I saw them all as my kinsfolk, I found in all of them the magic of the Name of Jesus. Sometimes I felt as light as though I had no body and was floating happily through the air instead of walking. Sometimes when I withdrew into myself I saw clearly all my internal organs, and I was filled with wonder at the wisdom with which the human body is made . . . And at all such times of happiness, I wished that God would . . . let me pour out my heart in thankfulness at His feet.

Thomas à Kempis ⋙
LOVE

O my Lord God, most faithful Lover, when You come into my heart, all within me rejoices. You are my glory and the joy of my soul, my hope and my whole refuge in all my troubles.

Love is a great and good thing; it alone makes burdens light and bears in equal balance things pleasing and displeasing. Love endures every hardship and does not feel it, and love makes bitter things tasteful and sweet. The noble love of Jesus perfectly imprinted in man's soul makes him do great things, and stirs him always to desire perfection . . .

Nothing is sweeter than love; nothing higher, nothing stronger, nothing larger, nothing more joyful, nothing fuller, nothing better in heaven or on earth; for love descends from God, and may not finally rest in anything lower than God. One with such love flies high; he runs swiftly, he is merry in God, he is free in soul. He gives all for all, and has all in all, for he rests in one high Goodness above all things, from whom all goodness flows . . .

Thomas à Kempis ⁂

LOVE

Love wakes much and sleeps little and, even in sleeping, does not sleep. It faints yet is not weary; it is restricted in its liberty yet is in great freedom. It sees reason to fear, yet does not fear, but, like an ember or a spark of fire, flames always upward, by the fervor of its love, toward God, and through the special help of grace is delivered from all perils and dangers.

He who is thus a spiritual lover knows well what that voice means which says: You, Lord God, are my whole love and desire. You are all mine, and I all Yours. Dissolve my heart into Your love so that I may know how sweet it is to serve You and how joyful it is to praise You, and to be as though I were all melded into Your love. Oh, I am urged on by love and go far above myself because of the great fervor I feel through Your unspeakable goodness. I shall sing to You the song of love; I shall follow You, my Beloved, in flights of thought wherever You go, and my soul will never be weary in praising You with the joyful songs of unconditional love.

Jean Pierre de Caussade

THE SACREDNESS
OF EVERY MOMENT

Come, all you simple souls—
    those without piety, grand talents,
    or lessons learned.

Come, all you
    who understand nothing of spiritual terms,
    who are filled with amazement
        at the eloquence of the learned.
Come, and I will teach you the secret,
    unreachable by those brilliant scholars—
The secret of perfection.
You will find this perfection within you,
    above you,
    below you,
    with every step you take.
Then you will be united with God—
    hand in hand you will walk.

Come, not to study the map of spiritual terrain,
But to possess it for yourself;
    To walk about in it
    without fear of going astray.

Why learn the theory of Divine Grace,
    and what it has been doing throughout the ages,
    when you can become and be the very instrument
    of its operation?

Come, not to discuss
    the words of others,
But to listen . . .
For in the sacredness of every moment
Divine Grace is telling you alone
    all that is required.

Jean Pierre de Caussade ⋙

COMPLETE ABANDONMENT
TO THE WILL OF GOD

The essence of all spirituality is this: "Complete and utter abandonment to the Will of God."

We must offer ourselves to God like a clean, smooth canvas and not worry ourselves about what God may choose to paint on it, but at each moment, feel only the stroke of His brush . . . It is the same with a piece of stone. Each blow from the sculptor's chisel makes it feel—if it could—as if it were being destroyed. As blow after blow descends, the stone knows nothing of how the sculptor is shaping it. All it feels is a chisel chopping away at it, cutting it, and mutilating it. For example, let's take a piece of stone destined to be carved into a crucifix or a statue. We might ask it: "What do you think is happening to you?" And it might answer: "Don't ask me. All I know is that I must stay immobile in the hands of the sculptor . . . I have no idea what he is doing, nor do I know what he will make of me. But I know his work is the best possible. It is perfect and so I welcome each blow of his chisel as the best thing that could happen to me, although, if I'm to be truthful, I feel that every one of these blows is ruining me, destroying me, and disfiguring me."

Jean Pierre de Caussade ⇝

A PURE HEART

O Lord, let others ask for every kind of gift, with more and more prayers; I ask for one gift with but one prayer: "Grant me a pure heart!" How blessed are the pure of heart. By the power of their faith they see God within themselves; they see Him above and below, in all things, at all times. They become the instruments of this Divine Play, as God guides them everywhere and leads them to everything.

A pure heart and good will! The one foundation of every spiritual state! . . . The pure heart could well say to every soul: "Look at me carefully. It is I who generate that love which always chooses the better part. I produce that mild but effective fear which arouses such a dread of wrong-doing that it can easily be avoided. I impart that excellent understanding which reveals the greatness of God and the merit of virtue. And it is also I who causes that passionate and holy yearning which keeps the soul resolute in virtue and in expectation of God."

Yes, O Pure Heart, you can invite everyone to gather round you and enrich themselves with your inexhaustible treasures. There is not one single kind of spiritual practice, not one path to holiness, which does not find its source in you.

Jean Pierre de Caussade ❧

FAITH

Faith transforms the earth into a paradise.
By it our hearts are raised with the joy
    of our nearness to heaven.
Every moment reveals God to us.
Faith is our light in this life.
By it we know the truth without seeing it,
    we are put in touch with what we cannot feel,
    recognize what we cannot see,
    and view the world stripped of all its outer shell.
Faith unlocks God's treasury.
It is the key to all the vastness of His wisdom.
The emptiness of all created things is disclosed by faith,
    and it is by faith
    that God reveals Himself . . .

With faith,
All that is dark becomes light,
    and what is bitter becomes sweet.
Faith transforms ugliness into beauty,
    and malice into kindness.
Faith is the mother of tenderness,
    trust, and joy . . .

There is nothing faith cannot overcome;
It passes beyond all shadows
    and through the darkest clouds
    to reach the truth, which it embraces
    and can never be parted from.

Jean Pierre de Caussade ❧

LOVE'S CALL

Come, then, my beloved souls,
    let us fly to that love which calls us.
Why are we waiting?
Let us set out at once,
Let us lose ourselves in the very heart of God
    and become intoxicated with His love.
Let us snatch from His heart the key
    to all the treasures of the world
    and start out right away on the road to heaven.
There is no need to fear
    that any lock will hold us back.
Our key will open every door.
There is no room we cannot enter.
We can make ourselves free of the garden,
    the cellar, and the vineyard as well.
If we want to explore the countryside,
    no one will hinder us.
We can come and go;
We can enter and leave anyplace we wish,
Because we have the key of David,
    the key of knowledge,
    and the key of the abyss
    that holds the hidden treasures
    of divine wisdom.
It is this key that opens the doors of mystical death
    and its sacred darkness.
By it we can enter the deepest dungeons
    and emerge safe and sound.
It gives us entrance into that blessed spot
    where the light of knowledge shines
    and the Bridegroom takes His noonday rest.

There we quickly learn how to win His kiss
   and ascend with surety the steps
   of the nuptial couch.
And there we learn the secrets of love—
Divine secrets that cannot be revealed
   and which no human tongue can ever describe.

Jean Pierre de Caussade ⚛

GOD'S TREASURE

What is the secret of finding this treasure? There isn't one. This treasure is everywhere. It is offered to us all the time and wherever we are. All creatures, friends or foes, pour it out in abundance, and it flows through every fiber of our body and soul until it reaches the very core of our being. If we open our mouths they will be filled. God's activity runs through the universe. It wells up around and penetrates every created being. Where they are, there it is also. It goes ahead of them, it is with them and it follows them. All they have to do is let its waves sweep them onward, fulfill the simple duties of their religion and state, cheerfully accept all the troubles they meet, and submit to God's will in all they have to do . . . This is the true spirituality, which is valid for all times and for everyone. We cannot become truly good in a better, more marvelous, and yet easier way than by the simple use of the means offered us by God: the ready acceptance of all that comes to us at each moment of our lives.

The Poet-Saints of India

INDIA IS A LAND BRIMMING WITH GOD'S PRESENCE: the air is thick with the ringing of temple bells, the chanting of God's Name, and the smell of incense issuing from the shrines and temples that dot every village, town, and city. Although the Indian scriptures hold that there is only one God, the religious practice of India embraces the worship of many different aspects of God. God is omnipotent; He has the power to create the entire universe and He also has the power to create forms or embodiments of Himself. Mankind cannot relate to, nor love, a formless Absolute. So, out of His compassion, God embodied Himself, and His aspects, into many forms. And it is through love and devotion to these forms or aspects of God that a worshiper can come to know God in His totality. The treasure of India, however, is not only found in her temples and her many forms of God, but in her Saints—those who have found God living within their own hearts, and who can lead people back to their own divinity.

Shankaracharya (686–718) was a Saint who completely renewed the practice of Hinduism and established monastic orders in the four corners of India. His vast literary output includes poems, hymns, scriptural commentaries, and the great philosophical treatise called *The Crest-Jewel of Discrimination*. After writing hundreds of books, and commenting on dozens of scriptures, Shankaracharya summed up his teaching as follows: "I can tell you the contents of a half million verses on spirituality in half a verse: God is real, the world is unreal, the individual soul is none other than God."

Kabir (15th century) is hailed as one of India's greatest exponents of devotional poetry. His powerful and inspired songs helped fuel India's *Bhakti* movement—a movement emphasizing devotion to God and the chanting of His Name. Even today Kabir's words can be heard echoing throughout the cities and villages of India and Pakistan. One scholar writes: "In the whole sweep of north Indian religion there is no voice more stringent, more passionate, more confident than that of Kabir."

Kabir was uneducated and spent most of his life as a poor weaver in the back streets of Benares. He was not of the proper class to have a Guru or receive any teachings on spirituality, yet his poetry is filled with mystical insights and profound teachings which baffled the great pundits of his time. Kabir's profound insights into truth, philosophy, and the nature of man came about from his direct experience of God—an experience that went beyond the ken of the intellect and worldly knowledge.

One major theme in Kabir's teaching revolved around the repetition of God's Name (*japa*). Kabir rejected all outer religious practice—and one reason why Kabir emphasized repeating God's Name was that this powerful practice was available to all people of all classes.

Tukaram (?1598–?1650) was born into a family of poor and unlearned peasants. Thanking God for this humble birth, he writes: "Well done, Lord! Had I been a learned man, pride and arrogance would have taken over and I would have scorned the service of the saints." Simple and direct, he was one of the great devotional poets of India.

Mirabai (1498–1546) was a Rajasthani princess famed for her love of Lord Krishna. Her "God-intoxicated" singing and dancing were considered a disgrace by her royal relatives, and legend has it that they repeatedly tried to kill her. By the power of her devotion, however, and by seeing everything as a gift from her Lord—even poison—she was always protected and all attempts on her life failed.

Akkamahadevi (12th century) was also oppressed by her royal surroundings and yearned for union with her Lord. She eventually renounced all her possessions, abandoned societal constraints, and wandered about with only her tresses as a covering. Her poems address three main forms of love—love withheld, love in separation, and love of union—all in praise and devotion to her chosen form of Lord Shiva, "the Lord White as Jasmine."

Ramdasa (1608–1681), the "Saint-errant," was an activist and the famed Guru of King Shivaji. His writings are brilliant and bold, praising the company of Saints and the greatness of God.

The "King of Saints" was **Jnaneshwar** (?1271–1293), who, while living only twenty-two years, made an indelible mark on the whole of Hindu spirituality. Before Jnaneshwar's time, the scriptures of India were in the secret language of Sanskrit and completely unavailable to the lower classes. Breaking from tradition, Jnaneshwar not only translated the central Sanskrit text, the *Bhagavad Gita*, into the common language of Marathi but added a magnificent commentary which expounds the complete path of yoga and spiritual practice. His commentary, the *Jnaneshwari*, still stands among the greatest spiritual works ever written.

Swami Muktananda (1908–1982) was a Saint from Ganeshpuri, India, whose writings capture the essence of Indian spirituality. Although the words of great Masters are invaluable, Muktananda's greatest contribution will no doubt be his bringing the secret, and experience, of *Shaktipat* (the awakening of one's *kundalini* energy) to the West. He also established the present form of *Siddha* yoga—a yoga based on chanting, meditation, service, and one's relationship to a perfect Master—which is practiced in ashrams and centers throughout the world.

Shankaracharya

The treasure I have found cannot be described in words,
the mind cannot conceive of it.
My mind fell like a hailstone into that vast expanse
of Consciousness.
Touching one drop of it I melted away and became one
with the Absolute.
And now, though I return to human consciousness,
I see nothing, I hear nothing,
I know that nothing is different from me.

Shankaracharya

What is the best thing a spiritual seeker can do?
  Carry out the instructions of his Guru.

What is the first and most important duty
  for a man of right understanding?
  To cut through the bonds of worldly desire.

To whom do the gods pay homage?
  To one who is compassionate.

Who is deaf?
  One who does not listen to good advice.

Who is dumb?
  One who does not speak kind words when they are needed.

What is most deplored?
  Miserliness in the wealthy.

Wherein lies strength?
  In patience.

Who profits from his life?
  One who is humble.

Who is free from sin?
  One who chants the name of God.

Shankaracharya

I am neither the mind, the intellect, nor the silent voice within;
Neither the eyes, the ears, the nose, nor the mouth.
I am not water, fire, earth, nor ether—
I am Consciousness and Bliss.
   I am Shiva! I am Shiva!

I am not the life-force nor the vital airs;
Not the seven components nor the five sheaths.
I am not the tongue, hands, feet, nor organ of procreation—
I am Consciousness and Bliss.
   I am Shiva! I am Shiva!

Neither attachment nor aversion can touch me;
Neither greed, delusion, pride, nor jealousy are mine at all.
I am not duty, nor wealth, nor happiness—
I am Consciousness and Bliss.
   I am Shiva! I am Shiva!

I am not virtue nor vice; not pain nor pleasure;
I am neither temple nor holy word; not sacred fire nor the
    Vedas—
I am Consciousness and Bliss.
   I am Shiva! I am Shiva!

I have neither death, nor doubt, nor class distinction;
Neither father nor mother, nor any birth at all.
I am not the brother, the friend, the Master, nor the disciple—
I am Consciousness and Bliss.
   I am Shiva! I am Shiva!

I am not detachment nor salvation,
   nor anything reached by the senses;

I am beyond all thought and form.
I am everywhere, and nowhere at all—
I am Consciousness and Bliss.
    I am Shiva! I am Shiva!

Kabir ⚛

THE BREATH WITHIN THE BREATH

Where do you seek me, my son?
Look—I am right inside you!
I am not found in the temple nor the mosque,
    not in Mecca nor the highest heaven.
I am not found in prayer nor ritual,
    not in yoga nor renunciation.
If your yearning is pure
    you will see me in an instant,
    you will meet me this moment.
Kabir says, "O seeker,
    I am right here—
    as the breath within the breath."

Kabir ⚛

THE SWING OF CONSCIOUSNESS

Between the pillars of spirit and matter
    the mind has put up a swing.
There swings the bound soul and all the worlds
    with not even the slightest rest.
The sun and moon also swing,
    and there is no end to it.
The soul swings through millions of births
    like the endless circling of the sun and moon.
Billions of ages have passed
    with no sigh of relief.
The earth and sky swing,
Wind and water swing,
Taking a body, God Himself swings.

Kabir, the servant of God,
has seen it all.

Kabir ⁂

O brother seekers!
Only while you are alive is there hope of finding Him.
While you are alive, meditate.
While you are alive, contemplate.
Only while you are alive can liberation be found.

If you do not cut the noose of your *karma* while living,
    what hope is there of liberation when you are dead?
It is a hopeless dream
    to think that union will come
    after the soul leaves the body.
What you get now
    is what you get then—
Otherwise, all you get is a stay in hell.
Embrace the real,
Recognize the true Guru,
Have faith in the power of the Name!
Kabir says,
    "Only spiritual practice will get you across;
    be addicted to this practice."

Kabir

The shadows of evening grow deep
    while love comes in to
    soothe every mind and body.

Look out toward the last glow of sunlight
    and look in
    to an endless sky.
Drink the nectar from the petals of your heart
    and let wave upon wave
    sweep through your body.
What glory in that ocean!
Listen!
    The sound of conches!
    The sound of bells!
Kabir says, "O brother, listen!
    The Lord of all
    plays His song within you!"

Kabir ❧

O swan, tell me your ancient tale
    of the land from which you come
    and of the shore to which you fly.
Where will you find refuge, O swan?
Where will you hold your hope?

Right now! This morning!
O swan, wake up!
Come with us to that place
    where there is no sorrow or doubt,
    where the passage of time cannot touch you.

In that place the forests are blooming with love,
    bursting with the fragrance of your own truth.
This is where the bumblebee of the mind
    has found its nectar,
    where it seeks no other joy.

Tukaram ≋

Now the unending treasure
   is laid open to all—
Come, take, and be rich.

Do not argue as to where
   that treasure may be
Or what jewels lie therein—
Come, take, and be rich.

Soon, like a pot broken and worn,
   this body will grow old.
But what the Master gives
   is ever new—
Come, take, and be rich.

No miserly doling of gifts with Him.
Like the flood of water in a drought,
All that your deepest soul needs
   is here for the taking—
Come, take, and be rich.

Tukaram ⌇

The Saint becomes so unified with God,
   that it is impossible to distinguish
   between God and Saint.
Embrace meets embrace.
Body is unified with body.
Words mix with words.
Eyes meet with eyes.

I have girded up my loins,
   and found a way
   to cross the ocean of life.
Come here, come here,
   great and small,
   women and men.
Take no thought; have no anxiety.
I shall carry all of you to the other shore.
I come as the sole bearer of the stamp of God
   to carry you over with His Name.

Tukaram ❧
GOD'S NAME

He who utters the Name of God while walking
   gets the merit of a sacrifice at every step.
His body becomes a place of pilgrimage.
He who repeats God's Name while working
   always finds perfect peace.
He who utters the Name of God while eating
   gets the merit of a fast
   even though he has taken his meals.
Even if one were to give in charity
   the whole earth encircled by the seas
   it would not equal the merit of repeating the Name.
By the power of the Name
   one will know what cannot be known,
One will see what cannot be seen,
One will speak what cannot be spoken,
One will meet what cannot be met.
Tuka says,
   Incalculable is the gain that comes
   from repeating the Name of God.

Tukaram ≫

When one looks into a mirror
  it seems as if one is looking at a different object,
  yet one is looking at oneself.
I am the brook that has merged into the river.
My country is now the whole universe.

Liberation cannot be purchased in a marketplace,
  nor can it be acquired
  by wandering in the woods or forest.
Liberation cannot be had by large quantities of wealth,
  nor can it be found in the upper or nether worlds.
Liberation can be acquired,
  says Tuka,
    only at the cost of life.

Mirabai ≫

O Bountiful Lord,
    Listen!
Can't you hear my prayer?
Can't you hear your Name
    upon my lips?

My whole family has turned against me
    and I am only a burden to them.
In all the worlds
    I have no one but you
    to call my own.

O Lord,
    steer my tiny boat—
    the waters are dark and stormy.
I cannot find rest until you come to me.
The nights are endless—
    I lie in my bed,
    without chance of sleep.
Open your door,
    I beg you.
The shaft of separation
    has split open my breast
    and the pain will not leave
    for even a moment.

Did you not restore life to Ahalya,
    frozen in stone by a sage's curse?
Beneath your magic touch,
    she raised up,
    and blossomed with beauty.
Why then don't you come and raise me up?
Am I not lighter than a statue of stone?

Mirabai ☙

You alone can break the chord
    that binds us now—
No one but you.
O Krishna,
You are the tree,
    I am the bird that nests in your branches.
You are the ocean,
    I am the fish that swims in your depths.
You are the hill,
    I am the peacock that dances on your top.
You are the full moon,
    I am the *chakor* bird
    that never turns its gaze from your light.
You are the gold,
    I am the rubbing powder that makes you shine.
O my Master,
    You are the Lord of the three worlds,
I am Mirabai,
    the one who sings your song,
    hoping you will hear me.

Mirabai ⫸

In whichever direction I look
I find the landscape full of Krishna,
    the Lord of Dark Blue.

The bowers and groves are dark,
The water of the Jamuna is dark,
The sky is overcast with dark clouds.
All colors are permeated with dark color.
People say this is something novel.
Am I mad, or have the dark pupils
    in the people's eyes changed?

The heart of the Moon
    and the scion of the Sun are dark;
The Musk is dark,
Kama, the conqueror of the world, is dark.
The neck of the blue-necked Shiva is also dark,
As if the dark color has been spread
    all over the earth.

The letters of the Vedas appear dark.
The point of the tapering light is also dark.
Not to speak of men and gods,
The Formless Brahman itself
    has assumed a dark form.

Mirabai ❧

O Beloved,
    Let us go to that place,
    Let us go there together.

Tell me, what should I wear?—
    A golden sari
    with a yellow flower behind my ear?
Or shall it be a simple dress
    with a string of pearls
    along the part of my hair?

Let me be your handmaid.
I will plant myself in your garden
    and there I will look upon your face
    and sing your praises forever.
Let me be your servant
    and let my only wages
    be the sweetness of your Name.

I have dreamt of you
    since the world began,
With a crown of peacock feathers on your head,
With robes of amber and yellow.
I see a garland of roses around your neck
    as you take the cows out to graze.

O Krishna,
    Charmer of hearts,
    Lifter of mountains,
I hear your flute calling me—
Shall I come by the secret path
    through the tall grass?

O Lord of Heavenly Blue,
My heart cannot rest until we are together,
   until we walk along the banks of the Jamuna
   deep into the night.

Akkamahadevi ⫸

WHITE AS JASMINE

You are the forest.
You are all the trees
   growing in the forest.
You are the birds and animals
   playing among the trees.

O Lord, White as Jasmine
When you are in everything, and everything is in you,
Why don't you show me your face?

Akkamahadevi

PERFECT LIGHT

It was like a flood of water
    pouring into the dry bed
    of a lake.
Like a torrent of rain
    quickening the plants
    once parched and lifeless.

It was like the pleasure of the world
    and the path to liberation,
    both rushing toward me.

Seeing the face of the Master,
    my Lord White as Jasmine,
    I became that perfect light.

Ramdasa

BRAHMAN

Brahman is before all things.
It fills the whole universe.
Nothing compares to its purity.
In all the heavens, in the celestial worlds,
    from the far reaches of the earth,
    it fills every nook and cranny.
It fills all this space at once.
It touches all and abides in all.
It cannot be soiled by clay.
It cannot be carried away by flood.
Simultaneously, it is before us and behind us.
Simultaneously, it is to our right and to our left.
Simultaneously, it is above and below.

As soon as we begin to be aware of it,
    we forget it.
But as soon as we forget it,
    it comes within the ken
    of our consciousness . . .

When we try to realize it,
    it cannot be realized.
When we try to leave it,
    it cannot be left.
We are connected with Brahman forever,
    and nothing can break this connection.

Ramdasa ≫

BRAHMAN

Brahman is more spotless than the sky.
It is formless and vast.
It extends above all heavens.
It exists beyond all worlds.
It occupies the smallest part of the universe.
It is quite near to us
    and yet it is hidden.
We live in it
    and yet we do not know it.

Wherever you cast your glance,
    it is before you.
You in fact see within it.
It is both inside and outside.
Where we feel it is not,
    it immediately manifests itself.
Whatever object we take in hand—
    it is nearer to us than that.

Ramdasa says,
Only one who has had the spiritual experience
    can know this secret.

Ramdasa ⁂
THE IDEAL MAN

The Ideal Man loves to put forth effort,
    enters boldly on any enterprise,
    and does not shun work.
He can live in the midst of difficulties,
    and bear the brunt of action,
    yet keeps himself free of entanglement.

He is everywhere,
    and yet nowhere.

Like Atman, he hides himself.
    Nothing can take place without his mediation,
    yet he is not himself seen.

Those who follow the instructions of a wise man
    become wise.
That is the justification of the existence of a wise man.
He always supports the right cause
    and never gives himself to falsehood.
In the midst of difficulties, he knows the way out.

A man of courage is a great support to all.
This indeed is what he has become
    through the grace of God.

Ramdasa ❧

DEATH

Death does not take power into account. Death does not take wealth into account. Death does not take fame into account. Death does not say this is a King; Death does not say this is an Emperor. Death does not say this is a learned man. Death does not say this is a man of higher caste . . . Death does not take the gods into account. Death does not take the incarnations of God into account . . .

Gone are the people of great glory. Gone are the people who defied death for a long time. Gone are the people of great fame. Gone are the generals and all their spoils. Gone are the sons of noble families. The protectors of men have all passed away. The great teachers and philosophers have passed away. Gone are those who wielded a sword. Gone are those who have given in charity. Gone are those who have protected the people. Gone are the great assemblies of men. Gone are all the scholars; gone are all the renunciants . . .

All those are gone, says Ramdasa. Only those who have realized the Self, and become one with Him, have remained.

Ramdasa ⇛
THE GURU

Without a true Guru,
　　we cannot attain our intimate treasure.
Without the grace of the Guru,
　　one cannot realize the Self.
Contemplation and concentration,
devotion and worship,
　　are all useless
　　without the grace of the Guru.
Without the grace of the Guru,
　　one moves like a blind man, floundering,
　　falling into ditches as he wends his way.

All great men that have lived in bygone times,
All the Saints and Sages of old,
　　have attained realization
　　only by the power of the Guru.

In short,
Liberation can be attained
　　only by the help of a Guru
　　and in no other way.

Jnaneshwar ⚜

I honor the God and the Goddess,
The eternal parents of the universe.

The Lover, out of boundless love,
    takes the form of the Beloved.
What beauty!
Both are made of the same nectar
    and share the same food.

Out of Supreme love
    they swallow up each other
But separate again
    for the joy of being two.

They are not completely the same
    but neither are they different.
No one can tell exactly what they are.

How intense is their longing
    to be with each other.
This is their greatest bliss.
Never, not even in jest,
Do they allow their unity
    to be disturbed.

They are so averse to separation
That even though they have become
    this entire world,
Never for a moment do they let a difference
    come between them.

Even though they see
    all that is animate and inanimate,

arising from within themselves,
They never recognize a third.

They sit together
    in the same place,
Both wearing a garment of light.
From the beginning of time
    they have been together,
Reveling in their own Supreme Love.

They created a difference
    to enjoy this world.
When that "difference" had one glimpse of their intimacy
It could not help
    but merge back into the bliss
    of their eternal union.

Without the God,
    there is no Goddess,
And without the Goddess,
    there is no God.

How sweet is their love!
The entire universe
    is too small to contain them,
Yet they live happily
    in the tiniest particle.

The life of one
    is the life of the other,
And not even a blade of grass can grow
    without both of them.

Only these two live
    in this house called the universe.
When either one is asleep

The other stays awake
    and plays the part of both.

Should both of them awake,
The whole universe would vanish
    without a trace.

They become two
    for the sake of a divine play,
But in every moment
    they seek to become one again.

Both of them see together,
Both of them are seen together.
They are happy
    only when together.

Shiva has become all forms:
    both dark and light,
    both male and female.
By the union of these two halves
    the whole universe comes to be.

Two lutes make one note.
Two roses make one fragrance.
Two lamps make one light.

Two lips—one word.
Two eyes—one sight.
Shiva and Shakti—one universe.

Though appearing separate
They are forever joined,
    always eating from the same plate.

She is a chaste and devoted partner;
   She cannot live without Her Lord.
And without Her,
   the one who can do everything
   cannot even appear.

How can we distinguish these two from each other?
He appears because of Her,
And She exists because of Him.

We cannot tell sugar
   from its sweetness,
Nor camphor
   from its fragrance.

To capture light
   we take hold of fire.
To capture the Supreme Shiva
   we must take hold of Shakti.

Light illumines the Sun,
But the Sun itself
   creates that light.
The glorious Sun and its light
   are one and the same.

An object has a reflection:
When looking we see two images,
   yet there is only one thing.
Likewise, this world is a reflection
   of the Supreme Lord.
We may see two,
Yet only One exists.

Out of pure emptiness
She gives rise to the entire world.
Everything depends on Her.

Yet She exists
only because of Her Lord.

Her form is the whole world,
it is the glory of God manifest.
God Himself created Her form,
God Himself became that form.

Seeing Herself beautifully adorned,
She could not bear that Her Lord
might have less than Herself.
And so She adorned Him
with every name and form in the universe.

Merged in unity
there was nothing to do.
So Shakti, the bringer of good fortune,
Created this world for the sake of divine play.

She reveals Her Lord's splendor
by melting Herself and becoming everything;
And He glorifies Her
by hiding Himself completely.

Out of His great love to see Her
He becomes the Seer of the universe.
If He could not watch Her play,
He would have no reason to exist.

To meet Her call
He takes on the form of the whole universe;
Without Her
He remains naked.

He is so mysterious and subtle,
That while apparent

He cannot be seen.
It is by Her grace alone
     that He comes into being.

She awakens Her Lord,
     and serves Him a feast the size of the universe.
With great delight
     He swallows up every dish
     and also the one who serves Him.

While He is sleeping,
She gives birth to all that exists
     and all that does not exist.
When She is sleeping,
     He has no form at all.

Look!
He is hidden,
     and cannot be found without Her.
For they are mirrors,
     each revealing the other.

Embracing Her,
Shiva enjoys His own bliss.
Though all the joy of the world belongs to Him,
There is no joy without Her.

She is His very form,
But Her radiance comes from Him.
Blending into one,
     they enjoy the nectar of their own union.

Shiva and Shakti are one,
Like air and the wind,
Like gold and its luster.

Shiva and Shakti cannot be separated.
They are like musk and its fragrance,
    like fire and its heat.

In the light of the Sun
    there is no difference between day and night.
In the Light of the Supreme Truth
    there is no difference between Shiva and Shakti.

Shiva and Shakti envy the Primordial Sound "Om"
    because they are seen as two
    while the sound Om is always regarded as one.

Jnanadeva says,
"I honor the union of Shiva and Shakti,
    who devour this world of name and form
    like a sweet dish.
All that remains is the One."

Embracing each other
    they merge into One,
As darkness merges with the light
At the breaking of dawn.

When we discover their Unity,
All words and all thoughts
    dissolve into silence,
Just as when the Universal Deluge comes,
    the waters of the ocean, and those of the Ganges,
    will merge into one . . .

The air and the wind
    will merge into the endless sky;
The sun and its light
    will merge into the Universal Fire.

With a true vision of them,
　　the seer and the seen
　　merge into one.
Again I honor
　　the two who are one.

They are like an ocean of knowledge.
And only those who throw themselves in can drink
　　of their waters.

I appear separate from them
　　just so I can honor them.
But that separation is not real,
　　it is only in name.

My praise is like that of a gold ornament
　　honoring the gold from which it is made.

When the tongue is used to pronounce the word "tongue,"
Is there any difference between the word
　　and the object meant by it?

One is called "ocean,"
　　the other is called "Ganges,"
　　and though these are different names,
Their waters are still the same.

The Sun can be seen,
　　but so can the objects it illumines.
Does this mean there are two Suns?
If moonlight shines on the surface of the Moon,
Or if the light of a lamp reveals the lamp,
　　can we claim that there is another?

The syllable "Om" is made up of the sounds A, U, and M,
　　does that mean it is divided?

The letter "N" is made up of three lines,
    does that mean it is more than one?

When the luster of a pearl
    shines upon its surface,
The pearl's beauty is only enhanced.

If one's bounty is not lessened,
    and only profit is obtained,
Why should the ocean not enjoy its waves,
    or a flower its own fragrance?

So I enjoy the worship of Shiva and Shakti,
    though I am never separate from them.

A reflected image disappears
    when the mirror is removed,
Ripples merge back into the water
    when the wind becomes still.

When sleep comes to an end,
    a man returns to his senses.
Now my individuality has come to an end,
    and I have returned to Shiva and Shakti.

Salt gives up its salty taste
    to become one with the ocean;
I give up my individual self
    to become Shiva and Shakti.

When the covering is removed,
    the air inside a plantain tree
    merges with the air outside.
And this is how I honor Shiva and Shakti—
    by removing all separation and
    becoming one with them.

Jnaneshwar

If I am concealed by the existence of the world,
Then who is it that blossoms in the form of the world?
Can a red jewel be concealed by its own luster?
Does a chip of gold lose its goldness if turned into an ornament?
Does a lotus lose itself when it blossoms into so many petals?
When a seed of grain is sown and grows into an ear of corn,
    is it destroyed or does it appear in its enhanced glory?
So there is no need to draw away the curtain of the world
    in order to see me,
        since I am the whole panorama.

Therefore, giving up the conception of difference,
a person should know Me alongside himself.
He should not regard himself as different from Me,
as a speck of gold is not different from the whole block of gold.
He should understand how a ray of light,
though proceeding from an origin,
is continuous with it.
Like molecules on the surface of the earth,
or flakes of snow on the Himalaya,
all individual souls dwell in Me.
A ripple, small or great, is not different from water.
So he should know himself as not different from Me.
Such insight is called Devotion.
This is the supreme knowledge, the essence of all Yoga.

Jnaneshwar ⚜
FINAL PRAYER

May the Self of the universe be pleased
With this sacrifice of words
And bestow His grace upon me.

May sinners no longer commit evil deeds,
May their desire to do good increase,
And may all beings live in harmony with one another.

May the darkness of sin disappear,
May the world see the rising of the sun of righteousness,
And may the desires of all creatures be satisfied.

May everyone keep the company of the saints devoted to God,
Who will shower their blessings on them.

Saints are the walking gardens
Filled with wish-fulfilling trees,
And they are the living villages
Of wish-fulfilling gems.
Their words are like oceans of nectar.

They are moons without blemish
And suns without heat.
May these saints be the friends of all people.

May all beings in the world be filled with joy,
And may they worship God forever . . .

Then the great Master said,
This blessing will be granted.
This brought great joy to Jnaneshwar.

Swami Muktananda ❧
THE GURU

If you understand what I am going to tell you, you won't have to work very hard, you won't even have to meditate very much. The Guru is not a physical form. The Guru is not an impressive figure peering at you from a picture. The Guru is not a person with long hair or a beard. The Guru is the divine power of Grace. The Guru is Shakti Herself. Even if you receive Shakti from the Guru, it is not his personal possession. The Shakti comes from the divine source, from the Supreme Lord, and this you must never forget.

If you do not have this knowledge, no matter how much you meditate, it will not lead you anywhere. If you are ignorant of the nature of Shakti, no matter how much wealth you have, you are poor. All that you need, wherever you are, is this constant awareness of the true nature of the Shakti, firm faith in it, and true devotion to it. If you have such firm faith, Shakti will guide you wherever you may be; Shakti will take the form of the Guru, or Shakti will give you messages from within. You will have absolutely no difficulty.

The world is a creation of Shakti, and a spiritual seeker, a meditator, should not look down upon the world or regard it as something other than Shakti. Shakti does not only manifest Herself as Divine Energy within the body; it is Shakti who projects the cosmos in the pure void. It is Shakti who makes this world while staying different from this world. It is Shakti who becomes good as well as bad. It is Shakti who manifests Herself in our worldly pursuits and also in our spiritual pursuits. So we should not regard our mundane life as being different from Shakti. That is an aspect of the same Shakti we are trying to attain through meditation. The Shakti creates the universe and dwells in a human being in the form of Divine Energy. A yogi worships Her and awakens Her. So nothing is really different or apart from the Shakti. Wherever you are you will receive guidance from the Shakti, because Shakti Herself manifests as your worldly life.

The state of a Siddha is beyond both knowing and not knowing. In that state, bliss is embraced by bliss. Joy is experienced through joy. Success is gained through success. Light dwells within light. . . . In that state, astonishment drowns in astonishment. All dos and don'ts are silenced. Rest attains total rest. Experience delights in experience. The state of a Siddha is the attainment of total perfection. Siddhas are like this. O friend, read this very carefully.

If a person with a taintless heart and a vigilant and pure mind keeps the company of a Siddha for just a moment, half a moment, or even half of that, he can instantly go across the ocean of mundane existence . . . Only by becoming a fish can one know how a fish lives. To understand a great being, one first has to become one with him. That is true knowledge.

This world is the beautiful Garden of Shiva, of the Lord, made so that you can walk in it with great joy. . . . Why do you find unhappiness in it? If there were no joy in this world, then God would not have created it with so much love and effort. So there is some mistake in your understanding and in your behavior—that is why when you look at the world you see unhappiness. So improve your vision, and then you will understand that the world is God.

God is everywhere, there's no doubt about that, but you have to have the right eye to see Him. Look at the air. It blows everywhere, but you can't see it. You can only feel it when it touches you. . . . God too can be seen. Sit quietly for a while and meditate on the Self. You'll be able to see Him. In what form would you like to see God? He has taken the form of bread in this piece of bread—don't try to see Him as a stone in bread. In fruit you should see God as fruit, in a tree you should see God as a tree, and in yourself you should see Him as yourself. Who says that God cannot be seen? Don't try to see Him as different from the way He has manifested Himself—see Him as He is! Try to see Him as He is.

Love is our only reason for living and the only purpose of life. We live for the sake of love, and we live seeking love. For the sake of love an actor performs, and for the sake of love a writer writes. For the sake of love a sensualist enjoys the pleasures of the body, and for the sake of love a meditator turns within and isolates himself from the world. Everything we do in life we do with the hope of experiencing love. We say, "If I do not find it today, perhaps I will find it tomorrow. If I do not find it in this person, perhaps I will find it in that one." Love is essential for all of us.

It is not surprising that we keep looking for love, because we are all born of love. We come out of love. All of us are nothing but vibrations of love. We are sustained by love, and in the end we merge back into love. . . . This world is nothing but a school of love; our relationships with our husband or wife, with our children and parents, with our friends and relatives are the university in which we are meant to learn what love and devotion truly are.

Yet the love we experience through other people is just a shadow of the love of the inner Self. There is a sublime place inside us where love dwells. . . . The love that pulses in the cave of the heart does not depend on anything outside. It does not expect anything. It is completely independent.

The love of the Self is selfless and unconditional. It is not relative. It is completely free. It is self-generated and it never dies. This kind of love knows no distinction between high and low, between man and woman. Just as the earth remains the same no matter who comes and goes on it, so true love remains unchanging and independent. Love penetrates your entire being. Love is Consciousness. Love is bliss. It does not exist for the sake of something else. It is supremely free. The path of inner love leads a lover to God. As a person walks on this inner path of love, he not only attains love, but merges in the ocean of love.

If you want to experience love, you have to start by loving yourself. First you have to love your body, then those who are related to your body, and then the master of the body, the inner Self. . . . The truth is that God has no physical body; the only body He has is the body of love. If the love you experience in your daily life—the little love you feel for your friends, your relatives, your pets, and even your possessions—could be turned toward the inner Self, that would be enough to bring you liberation.

Swami Muktananda

THE UNIVERSAL ENERGY (CHITI)

Chiti is supremely free. She is self-revealing. She is the only cause of the creation, sustenance, and dissolution of the universe. She exists, holding the power within Her that creates, sustains and destroys. The prime cause of everything, She is also the means to the highest bliss. All forms, all places, and all instants of time are manifested from Her. She is all-pervading, always completely full and of everlasting light. Manifesting as the universe, still She remains established in Her indivisibility and unity. Within the Blue Light, She pulsates as ambrosial bliss. There is nothing apart from Her. There is no one like Her. She is only One, the supreme witness, the One who is called cosmic consciousness or Supreme Shiva. She is ever solitary. In the beginning, in the middle, and in the end, only Chiti is. She does not depend on any other agency; She is Her own basis and support. As She alone exists, She is in perfect freedom.

Swami Muktananda ⫸
THE FINAL REALIZATION

As I gazed at the tiny Blue Pearl, I saw it expand, spreading its radiance in all directions so that the whole sky and earth were illuminated by it. It was now no longer a Pearl but had become shining, blazing, infinite Light; the Light which the writers of the scriptures and those who have realized the Truth have called the divine light of Chiti. The Light pervaded everywhere in the form of the universe. I saw the earth being born and expanding from the Light of Consciousness, just as one can see smoke rising from a fire. I could actually see the world within this conscious Light, and the Light within the world, like threads in a piece of cloth, and cloth in the threads. Just as a seed becomes a tree, with branches, leaves, flowers, and fruit, so within Her own being Chiti becomes animals, birds, germs, insects, gods, demons, men, and women. I could see this radiance of Consciousness, resplendent and utterly beautiful, silently pulsating as supreme ecstasy within me, outside me, above me, below me.

All philosophies and scriptures say the same thing: "God dwells in this human body."

Do not consider your body a mere lump of flesh made of seven components. It is a noble instrument. In it are situated all holy places, gods, *mantras*, and the source of all extraordinary powers in this world. . . . God dwells in the body. He is present as fully in you as in the highest Heavens. Why are you exhausting yourself looking for Him in different places instead of in your own heart? You should live your normal life, but accord Him the chief place among your daily activities. Whatever may be your religion or philosophy, do not make yourself a foolish, weak, and trivial creature. Do not head toward decline and disaster by regarding this body as godless. Do not commit spiritual suicide by belittling yourself through defective understanding.

There are many different phenomena inside the human body. If a man were to see the inner splendor in meditation even once, he would derive immense benefit from it. How wonderful the treasures within this body! Pools of nectarean juices! Numberless sheaves of sensory nerves! Reverberating musical concerts! Varied intoxicating perfumes! Countless rays of different suns! Sacred dwellings of gods! In spite of such wealth, man goes looking for sweet happiness in the external world and ends up weary and joyless.

The universe within is superior to that without. How wonderful the seat of clairaudience in the ear! How significant the center of deep sleep in the throat, which easily dissolves the fatigue of the waking hours. . . . In your heart there is a lotus whose different petals stand for different qualities such as anger, infatuation, greed, love, modesty, knowledge, joy, and so on. Sages have spent their whole lives trying to behold the scintillating divine light that lies within the heart. How glorious the Goddess Kundalini who transforms a man as She expands. O soul of man! What joy could beckon you in the external world while such an infinite treasure of marvels lies within?

When the latent treasure of inner Shakti is released in meditation, you will soon ascend to the higher stages of meditation. You will see splendid sights and glorious forms. You will perceive internal divine lights. It is only by virtue of these lights that your body becomes beautiful and you feel love for one another. As the magnificent radiance sparkles in meditation, your craving for beautiful and loving forms will be satisfied. You will see the whole world as radiant.

Along with visions, you will hear inner sounds. Sweet, divine music will ring in your ears. As you listen to it, you will have such a sleep as is enjoyed only by heavenly beings. These melodious strains will compel you to dance in ecstasy and eradicate your indifference, distress, and ramblings of mind. Not only this, the inner music will release celestial ambrosia and you will relish its sweetness. This nectar, trickling from the palate, is the sweetest of all tastes. Each drop is worth more than millions. This elixir will expel all your diseases and fill you with gladness. Your anger will vanish. You will exude ambrosial sweetness. You will rejoice in your spouse and children. As you taste this nectar and become absorbed in it, you will be transported with inner delight.

O my dear ones! You will also inhale divine scents. As your inner aroma is released, not only your home but your whole world will become tranquil; your body will shed its heaviness and sloth, and become lithe and vibrant.

When your inner Kundalini Shakti is stirred, She will release Her impulses of love throughout your body and its seventy-two thousand nerves. She will thrill your every blood cell with Her ecstatic joy. Only then will your craving for touch be truly gratified. You will recover the lost luster of your eyes. Your withered face will again glow with love and your lips will become rosy. Your world will quiver with beauty, joy, and love! You will become aware of the omnipresence of the Lord; you will realize that this entire world is His and that He is maintaining it.

My dearest ones! Do not give up your worldly life, your near and dear ones. Do not waste yourselves away, rushing around in search of God in the four directions, nor lose your own souls while seeking inner peace and comfort. Live in your own homes with your spouses and children, making full use of your artistic talents, or running your businesses or factories. In whatever position your destiny has placed you, whether you are millionaires or laborers, kings or beggars, God belongs to you all. If you call Him with love, thinking about Him with devotion, He will reveal Himself to you. He will grant a vision of the divine light of His love. Then you will know that you are an embodiment of bliss. You will realize, "I am Shiva! Yes I am! Yes I am!"

A Note on the Translations

When bringing a spiritual work from one language to another, every level of translation must be considered. There is, of course, a literal translation, which is accurate and true to the words, yet often lacking the flavor or power of the original. Even literal translations, especially from the Chinese, can be extemely varied and highly subjective. On the other side, there are "spring-board" translations or renderings—popular among poetic types—where images and ideas from the original are borrowed to form the basis of a new poem. The translations and renderings found in this work fall somewhere between these two sides. Although I have honored the words and language of the original—attempting to preserve the flavor of a particular time and culture—I have often departed from the literal words in an attempt to capture the "spirit" and underlying pulse of the original. Although I have stayed close to the original in most cases, my loyalty has been to the writer's message, the expression of his or her heart, and not the literal words used.

A successful translation of a spiritual work does not always require access to the original language—though this is often indispensable—but it always requires access to one's own spirit, and the ability to find that place within oneself where the original words arose. Through meditation and prolonged contemplation on the text, the would-be translator joins in an exalted state of fellowship with the original author—he begins to see as the original writer sees, and think as the writer thinks. Once this "discovery" has taken place, the translator must ask himself, "How would the original writer convey these ideas to us now? What words would he use, in our language?" It is by translating from this perspective, and this awareness, that the translator is able to restore the original power to the sacred words of spiritual masters.

Three different terms are used when referring to works in this collection: "Translation" is used when the primary source for the work is a manuscript in the original language; "rendition" is used when the work is produced by rewording or reformulating one or more existing translations; "adaptation" is used when the work is produced by editing or correcting a single previous translation.

Verbatim and Literal Translations

"Transliteration" refers to a close representation of how a foreign word or character might sound when spelled out in the English alphabet. "Verbatim" refers to a word-per-word translation. "Literal" refers to a translation that closely reflects the words and meaning of the text, without elaboration or interpretation. Transliterations and verbatim translations from the Chinese (*Tao Te Ching*) by C. J. Ming; transliterations and verbatim translations from the Persian (Rumi) by Shahram Shiva; transliterations and verbatim translations from the Hindi (Kabir) by Krishan Bakshi and Vinod Argawal. All literal translations and notes by Jonathan Star.

TAO TE CHING (Chinese)
RUMI (Persian)
KABIR (Hindi)

TAO TE CHING, VERSE 14
(Translation on page 31)

shi	looking / perceive / gazing / [we] look / try to see // consider
chi	it / at it / that
pu	not / do not / cannot
chien	seen / see / perceive
ming	name
yueh	speak / call / say }} named / it is called / its name is
i	invisible / colorless / very dim // unobtrusive / elusive
t'ing	hearing / listening / [we] listen / try to hear
chi	to it / it
pu	not / do not / cannot
wen	heard / hear
ming	name
yueh	speak / call / say }} named / it is called / its name is
hsi	soundless / inaudible / very faint / the Inaudible / rarefied
poh	grasp / grab / touch / try to touch / reach for
chi	it
pu	not / do not / cannot
teh	obtain / catch / get hold of

ming	name
yueh	speak / call / say }} named / it is called
wei	formless / minute / fading away / subtle / bodiless
ts'z	these
san	three
che	things / (attributes / qualities / characteristics / properties)
pu	not / are not
k'o	can / able }} cannot be / elude / evade
chi	further / closer / reach the end
ch'ih	scrutinize / investigate / inquire
	}} be comprehended / fathomed / defined
ku	therefore / hence // for indeed / thus [they]
hun	merge / blend / mingle [together] / join / are fused
arh	and
wei	make / form / act as / become / (are fused into)
yih	one / a unity
ch'i	Its / (the One's)
shang	above / top part / upper side / surface // going up / rising
pu	is not
chiao	bright / light / dazzling / shine / clear
ch'i	Its
hsia	below / bottom / underside // coming down / setting / falling
pu	is not
mei	dark / dim / obscure
sheng	continuous / infinite / boundless // unbroken thread[1]
sheng	continuous / infinite / boundless // unbroken thread
pu	not
k'o	able to / can
ming	name }} unnameable / nameless
fuh	returns / reverts / (moves on)
kuei	return / revert / restore back / again
yü	to

1. **Sheng** refers to a cord, string, or line, especially one stretched taut. A stretched cord can be used to adjust a measurement, correct something out of line, or keep things in conformity with a single principle. A stretched cord can also be seen as an "unbroken thread" or something which is continuous or unending.

wu	non- / without
wuh	existence / being / things / substance
	}} nothingness / the realm of non-existence
shi	this is / therefore it is
wei	called
wu	without
chuang	form / shape / state
tzu	's / of / of its own
chuang	form / shape / state }}}} formless form
wu	without
wuh	existence / object / substance / things
chi	of its own
hsiang	figure / image / image }}}} imageless image
shi	thus / therefore it is
wei	called
hu	vague / obscure / indistinct / elusive / blurred / indefinable
huang	evasive / elusive / unimaginable / indistinct / shadowy
ying	front // meeting / going toward / encounter / stand before
chi	it
pu	not / do not / [you will] not
chien	see / discover / perceive
ch'i	its
sheu	head / face / front / (beginning)
sui	follow / follow behind / go after
chi	it
pu	not / do not / [you will] not
chien	see / discover / perceive
ch'i	its
heu	back / rear / (end)
chih	hold / grasp / seize / stay with / [he who] holds fast
ku	ancient / of old / the ancients / way of antiquity
chi	(of) / 's / its
tao	Tao / way
i	in order to / so as to / thereby / to
yü	govern / manage / control / direct / steer / master / harness
chin	the present
chi	(of) / its
yiu	existence / realities / things

neng	able to / can / have the power to
chi	know / understand [its / it as]
ku	old / primeval / ancient / first
shi	beginning / origin
shi	this is // here indeed
wei	called
tao	Tao's
chi	"main thread" / unbroken strand // bond / lineage / tradition²

TAO TE CHING, VERSE 29

(Translation on page 33)

tsiang	take in hand / receive // will / if / when going to
yü	tendencies / habits / desires / wants to / thought constructs
ts'ü	take / take over / conquer / govern / take hold of
t'ien	heaven
hsia	below }} the world / the empire / (natural world)
erh	and / but
wei	act / make / do / act upon / do anything to//
	"impose an order on things alien to their inner rhythm"
chi	it / he / she / them
wu	I
chien	recognize / perceive / discover / see / know / think
ch'i	him / she / it
pu	not / no / cannot
teh	succeed / success / achieve / obtain / gain / benefit / get
	}} "cannot be done" / fail
i	end / cease / finish / decline / "that is all"
	}}} won't reach the end / won't finish
t'ien	heaven
hsia	below
shan	sacred / soul / spirit / divine / transcendent / "most sublime"
	Lit: "extend" + "heaven" ("the extension of heaven")

2. **Chi** denotes tradition, discipline, principle, order, etc. It refers to a system, principle, or continuity that binds things together.

ch'i	vessel / bowl / utensil / thing / entity
pu	not / no / nothing
k'o	can / able / should }} should not be
wei	act upon / tampered with / contrived / control / try to change / make / made / act
ye	! / indeed
wei	acts upon / does anything to it / tampers / change / make
che	he / him / it / the one
pai	ruin[s] / destroy[s] / defect / mar / spoil / fail
chi	it / he / she
chih	holds / take hold of / grasp / seize // manage
che	he / she / the one
shih	lose / loses / lost / destroy / be separated from
chi	it / he / she
hu	thus / therefore / hence / for
wuh	things / beings / all this
ho	some / sometimes / likely / perhaps / (a time for) / (a time to)
hing	lead / go out / travel / ahead / go forward / step
huo	some / other / sometimes
sui	follow / follow behind / behind / imitate / comply with
huo	some / other / sometimes
hü	sigh / breathe out / blow hot / breathe gently
huo	some / other / sometimes
ch'ui	breathe in / blow cold / breathe hard
huo	some / other / sometimes
ch'iang	forceful / strong / [get] stronger / strength
huo	some / other / sometimes
lei	weak / weakness / thin / emaciated / decay
huo	some / other / sometimes
tsai	succeed / fill up / have a lot / overcome / be up / begin
huo	some / other / sometimes
hwui	fail / give in / succumb / fall / be down / be destroyed / end
shi	(therefore)
i	(therefore) / that is why / thus / hence
shang	holy
jan	man }} sage / the sage / sages
ch'ü	abandons / avoids / leaves / rejects / discards / gets rid of

shen	excess / extremes / "pleasures" / "over-doing"
ch'ü	abandons / avoids / leaves / rejects / discards / casts off
shen	extravagance / extravagant / elaborate
ch'ü	abandons / leaves / rejects / discards
tai	excessive / indulgence / "a life of excess" / extremes / arrogance

KABIR

(Translation on page 185)

TRANSLITERATION

Hamsa karo puratan baat
Kaun des se aayaa hamsa, utarnaa kaun ghat
Kahan hamsa bisaraam kiyaa hai, kahan lagaaye aas
Abahin hamsa chet sabera, chelo hamare sath
Samsaya-soka wahan nahin vyapai, nahin kal kai traas
Hiaan madana-bana phool-rahe-hain, aave soham baas
Man bhonra jihan arujh rahe hain, sukh ki naa abhilas

VERBATIM

Swan[1] | to do/make/share | ancient/enduring/endless[2] | tale/ conversation/(tell me)

Which/what | land/country | from | come | swan | attach/flying to/descending | which | riverbank/shore/*ghat*

Where | swan | settle/rest/(refuge) | did | is | where | attach/put | longing/hope

Now/right now | swan | wake up/become aware | morning | come | our | with

Doubt/uncertainty | sorrow | there | not/no | pervade/exist/extend | no/not | time/death | of | troubled/bothered

1. In the scriptures of India, the swan (*hamsa*) often refers to the individual soul (*jiva*), and its flight back to God. A peculiar quality of the swan, unlike other birds, is that it always flies alone.
2. Implies the tale of the human condition—the endless cycle of birth and death.

Here | the forest of Kamadev (god of love)/forest of desires[3] | is
flowering/blooming | [here] comes | "So'ham"/"I am That" / (aware-
ness of one's unity with God) |
fragrance mind | bumblebee | there | immersed/enjoying happiness |
of | no | desire

O swan, share with me your ancient tale.
From which country do you come, O swan? To what shore do you fly?
Where will you rest, O swan? Where do you hold your hope? (What do
you hope to find?)
Right now, this morning, O swan, wake up! Come with us.
[To a place] where neither doubt or sorrow exist (are spread out),
    where there is no more torment of death.
Here the forest of Madana (the god of love) is flowering,
    giving off the [sweet] scent of "So'ham."
[In that place] the bee of the mind is [so] absorbed (immersed in nectar)
    that it seeks no other happiness (i.e., outside itself)

KABIR
(Translation on page 182)

TRANSLITERATION
Jaha(n) chet-achet khambha dou mana rachyaa hai hindor
Tahan jhoolai(n) jeeva jahan, jaha(n) katahun nahin thir thaur
Aur chand-soor douu jhoolai nahin paavai anta
Chauraasee lachhu jiv jhoolai(n), jhoolai(n) ravi-sasi dhaya
Kotin kalpa jug beetiya aane na kabahun haaya
Dharni akaasahu douu jhoolai(n) jhoolai(n) pavanahun neer
Dhari deh hari aapahoo(n) jhoolai(n) jo lakhahei(n) dasa kabira

3. *Madana-bana* is the forest of Madana (Kamadev), the god of worldly
love and desire. This phrase can be seen to represent the world, where
desires play themselves out. Here the sense is more positive, suggesting
a place where all desires are fulfilled, where love is blooming everywhere.

Where | conscious/alive/spiritual-lacking consciousness/inert/matter[1] |
pillars | two | mind | created/put together | is | swing[2]
There | swing | individual soul/*jiva* | world | where | not even a speck/absolutely | no | permanent/steady | place
And | sun-and-moon | both | swing | not | attain | end (there is no end to it)
Eighty-four | 100,000/lakhs | soul/*jiva*[3] | swing | swing | sun-moon | happen
Crore/100 *lakhs*/billions | *kalpa*/1000 ages[4] | *yuga*[5]/age | passed/spent |
come | not | when ((never)) | a sigh of sorrow/(sigh of relief)
Earth | sky | both | swing | swing | wind/air | water
Taking | body | God/*Hari* | himself | swing | that | saw/describe/extol | servant/slave/*das* | Kabir

The mind has created two pillars, one of spirit one of matter, upon which
   it swings.
There swings the *jiva* and the whole world, with absolutely no steadiness.
And the sun and moon also swing, yet they don't attain/reach the end.
Where the soul swings through 84 *lakh* births/wombs, so swings the sun
   and moon.

1. *Chet-achet*, consciousness/lacking consciousness. This pair of opposites
also suggest the spiritual world and the physical world. *Chet* also means
something which is alive, infused with a dynamic energy—as opposed to
something inert and lifeless.
2. This swing relates to the dichotomy of *chet-achet*, spirit-matter, and
suggests the endless cycle of birth and death (*samsara*) whereby the individual soul "swings" back and forth between pure consciousness and
incarnated matter (the body). "Only when the false distinction between
matter and consciousness is exploded does the individual soul attain liberation from the cycle of birth and death."
3. According to Hindu evolutionary theory, there are eighty-four *lakhs*
(8.4 million) different species living on earth, through which the incarnated soul (*jiva*) must pass. Thus, this line could be interpreted as,
"Every creature on earth (contained in all the species) are swinging," or
"The soul has swung through 8.4 million births."
4. *Kalpa*, a day of Brahma (the Creator), which is just over 4 billion
years, and equal to half the duration of all creation.
5. There are four *yugas* or ages. We are now at the very beginning of the
Kali Yuga (the Dark Age), an age lasting for 432,000 years.

Millions of ages have passed, and never has there been a sigh of relief.
Earth and sky both, wind and water swing.
Taking a body, God/*Hari* himself swings.
Kabir, the servant of God, sees it all.

RUMI

(Translation on page 109)

TRANSLITERATION

Emrooz che roozast, ke khorsheed dotaast
Emrooz ze roozhaa, beroonast-o jodaast
Az charkh, bekhaakian nesaarast-o sedaast
Kei delshodegaan, mozhdeh, ke een rooz-e shomaast

VERBATIM

today / what [kind of] / day it is / that / the sun / is two
today / of days / is outside (different) and / it is separate
of / the wheel / to those on earth / is a call to a wedding and / a sound
that O / you who have become one with your hearts / good news / that
   / this / day / is for you

LITERAL

What kind of day is it today that there are two suns in the sky?
This day is different from other days.
The heavens are calling everyone on earth to the day of union with God.
How fortunate you are that you have become one with your own heart
   (/ that you can hear heaven's call), this is your day.

RUMI

(Translation on page 107)

TRANSLITERATION

Cheshmee daaram, hame por az soorat-e doost
Baa-deedeh ma-raa khosh ast, chon doost daroost
Az deedeh-o doost, farghkardan na nekoost
Yaa doost bejaaye deedeh, yaa deedah khodoost

these eyes / I have / all / full / of / face of the / Beloved
with the sight / to me / pleasing / it is / because / the Beloved / is in it
of / the sight and / the Beloved / to differentiate / is not / good, fitting
either / the Beloved / in the place of / the sight / or / the sight / is him

My eyes are filled with the sight of the Beloved. // Everywhere I look I
see the Beloved.

This sight is pleasing, because I see the Beloved. // I am happy to see my
Beloved everywhere.

It is not good to see the Beloved as being separate from what you see
(/ your own seeing).

The Beloved is your seeing (looks through your eyes) and all that you
see.

Glossary

Ananda (Sanskrit) ◆ Bliss. The bliss of God that permeates everything. The nature of the Absolute is often described as *Sat-Chit-Ananda* (Truth-Consciousness-Bliss). *Ananda* is used as an ending in the names of Indian monks: Anantananda (endless bliss), Sevananda (the bliss of selfless service), Nityananda (everlasting bliss), Muktananda (the bliss of freedom).

Arjuna (India, ?5th century B.C.) ◆ Famed archer and warrior prince to whom Lord Krishna imparted his teachings in the *Bhagavad Gita*.

Ashram (Sanskrit) ◆ From the Sanskrit *a*, "without," and *shram*, "fatigue." A place where discipline and spiritual practices are followed; the abode of a Guru or Master. A typical ashram schedule includes early morning meditation, chanting of sacred texts, selfless service (*seva*), and study of the truth (*satsang*).

Atman (Sanskrit) ◆ Divine Consciousness residing in the individual. The soul.

Bhakti (Sanskrit) ◆ Absorption, devotion, and love of God or one's Guru. It is honored as the most assured path to enlightenment and the support of all other spiritual practices. The definitive text on *bhakti* is *The Bhakti Sutras of Narada*, which states:

> *This Love is devoid of qualities, seeks no return, grows from more to more every moment, knows no break, is subtler than the subtlest and is of the nature of experience. Attaining this Love, the loving devotee sees nothing but Love, hears only about Love, speaks only of Love, and thinks of Love alone.*

Brahman (Sanskrit) ◆ The all-pervasive Absolute Reality; God.

Buddha (Sanskrit) ◆ Literally the "Awakened One," it is a Buddhist term for an enlightened being. It also refers to the historic founder of Buddhism, who lived in the 6th century B.C., and whose birth name was Siddhartha Gautama.

Chiti (Sanskrit) ✦ The ever-creative power of God; Consciousness in the form of the supreme energy which gives rise to the universe; *Shakti* (Sanskrit), *Sophia* (Greek).

Confucius (China, 551–479 B.C.) ✦ The most influential philosopher of China and founder of Confucianism, a humanistic approach to life which emphasizes the learning and practice of kindness to one's family and neighbors, and proper moral conduct.

Dharma (Sanskrit) ✦ From the Sanskrit root *dhr*, meaning "to sustain," "to uphold," "to nourish." *Dharma* is that which sustains life, the inherent laws of the world, and the divine order of the universe. It is most often associated with one's duty—how one sustains his own livelihood—however, on a deeper level, *dharma* refers to a life that is in harmony with the natural flow of the universe. *Dharma* is action that pleases the Lord; action which leads a soul to union with God—and this most often *is* one's duty in life. In the *Bhagavad Gita*, Lord Krishna says, "Devoted to one's duty, man obtains perfection."

Dharma is a universal concept and often translated as "virtue." The New Jerusalem Bible says: "Virtue is to be understood as perfect accord of mind and act with the divine will as manifested in the precepts of the law and injunctions of conscience." The Chinese called this perfect accord *Te*—the manifestation of Tao in a person and his actions; the Greeks used the word *eudaimonia*—"a good God within"; and the Hebrews *tsedeq*—"righteousness," the keeping of God's laws.

Although it is *dharmic* to carry out one's duty, the consummation of all *dharma*, the highest *dharma*, is to realize the Self. Anything that is contrary to this end cannot be true *dharma*.

Dhyana Yoga ✦ The yoga of meditation, which is based on focusing the mind on a given object, one's Guru, one's breath, or on the space between the breaths. Zen Buddhism has its roots in this form of yoga: the word *Dhyana* in Sanskrit became *Ch'an* in Chinese and later *Zen* in Japanese.

Guru (Sanskrit) ◆ From the Sanskrit *gu*, meaning "darkness," and *ru*, meaning "light." A Guru is a particular kind of enlightened being who has the power to dispel the darkness of ignorance with the light of the truth. The Grace bestowed by the Guru is the root of all attainments and realizations.

"He alone is the real Guru who leads a disciple to liberation" (Ramdasa).

"The Guru is totally established in the truth of Brahman and constantly acting for the benefit of his disciples" (Shankaracharya).

Hatha Yoga ◆ From the Sanskrit *ha* (sun) and *tha* (moon), *hatha* yoga is the practice of various mental and physical postures (*asanas*), and the control of breath, which purify the subtle channels of the nervous system, strengthen the body, calm the mind, and balance the solar and lunar life-forces (*prana*).

Japa Yoga ◆ The practice of absorbing one's mind in the continual repetition of God's Name. This yoga begins when a disciple receives a *mantra* or divine word from a Guru, i.e., from one who has realized the full power of the *mantra*. The continuous repetition of The Jesus Prayer by Christians, or the Name of Amida in the Pure Land School of Buddhism is a form of japa yoga.

For this practice to bear fruit, one must have complete faith in the power of the *mantra;* and no distinction should be made between the *mantra*, the one who repeats the *mantra*, and the Supreme Self.

On the power of the Name, Tukaram writes:

> *By the power of the Name of God, one shall come to know what one does not know. One shall come to see what cannot be seen. One will come to speak what cannot be spoken. One will come to meet what normally cannot be met. Incalculable is the gain which comes from repeating the Name.*

Karma (Sanskrit) ◆ From the Sanskrit root *kr*, "action," *karma* is any action of the body, mind, or speech, and the result of that action. The notion of *karma* is captured in the phrase: "As you sow, so shall you reap."

To every action there is a corresponding reaction. Every action based on the notion that one's action is one's own (as opposed to God being the root of all action)—be it good or bad action—binds one to this world. It is not through performance of good deeds but only through selfless service, renouncing the fruits of one's action, and seeing one's own actions as the actions of God that one is freed from the bonds of *karma*. However, the storehouse of *karma* accumulated in this lifetime and in previous lifetimes, is so vast that one must not only stop its creation but also "burn it up." Spiritual practices such as *mantra* repetition, chanting of God's Name, service to one's Master, and meditation on the Self all have the power to burn up the burden of past *karma*. (See **Karma Yoga**.)

Karma Yoga (Sanskrit) ◆ The yoga of selfless service (*seva*); acting without any sense of doership (i.e., seeing all one's actions as the actions of God); dedicating the fruits of one's actions to God. The *Bhagavad Gita* is the supreme text of *karma* yoga which says that man has the right to work but not to the fruits of his actions. In his commentary on the *Gita*, Jnaneshwar tells more about this mysterious yoga:

> When the sun rises and sets, it seems to move although it is actually motionless. In the same way, realize that freedom from action lies in action. Such a person seems like other people, but he is not affected by human nature, like the sun which cannot be drowned in water. He sees the world without seeing it, does everything without doing it, and enjoys all pleasures without being involved in them . . .
>
> The walking of his feet, the speaking of his mouth, and all his other actions are the Supreme moving through him. Furthermore, he sees the whole universe as not different from himself. So how can action affect him? . . . He is free in every way and, even though he acts, he is free from action. Though he possesses attributes, he is beyond all attributes. There is no doubt about this.

Krishna (India, ?5th century B.C.) ◆ From the Sanskrit meaning "the dark one," or "the one who attracts irresistibly," Krishna was an incarnation of God who came to reestablish righteousness in the world. Krishna is one of the most beloved deities of India, and countless love poems have been written to, and about, Krishna. His life is described in the Indian scripture the *Srimad Bhagavatam*, and his teachings on yoga, given to Arjuna on the battlefield, are contained in the *Bhagavad Gita*.

Kundalini (Sanskrit) ◆ From the Sanskrit meaning "the coiled one," the *kundalini* is a particularized form of the creative energy of the universe (*Shakti*) that lies coiled, or dormant, at the base of the *sushumna* in the subtle body (corresponding to the spinal cord in the physical body). This power is contained in seed form in every human being. Once this "serpent energy" is awakened (through the grace of a Master), it journeys up through the central channel of the subtle body—removing all physical, mental, and spiritual blocks—and finally enters the spiritual center in the crown of the head. Once this happens the individual self merges with the universal Self and realization is attained.

Mahabharata (Sanskrit) ◆ The great epic poem of India that tells of the establishment of *dharma* (righteousness) in the world through the legendary account of two sides of a family at war. Its most famous part is Lord Krishna's telling of the *Bhagavad Gita* to Arjuna.

Mansur Mastana (Persia, 858–922) ◆ A Sufi Saint from Bhagdad who was hanged as a heretic by the orthodox of Islam for his proclamation *Ana'l haq*, "I am God."

Mantra (Sanskrit) ◆ A sacred word or sound infused with the power of God. When a *mantra* is repeated, it draws that power into the one who repeats it. The *mantra* can be seen as a Name of God, and the Supreme Being in the form of sound.

Correct repetition of a *mantra* is not only the repetition of a sacred word, but the continual awareness that the Guru who imparted the *mantra*, the one repeating the *mantra*, the *mantra* itself, and the Supreme Lord are one and the same. Only with this awareness will the *mantra* have the power to purify, protect, redeem, and ultimately give realization to the one who repeats it.

A *mantra* given by a Guru is a form of initiation called *mantra diksha*: for through the *mantra*, the power of God enters a disciple and—when the disciple repeats the *mantra*—it gives him access to this supreme power. This form of *mantra* is "alive": it purifies, protects, redeems, and ultimately gives realization to the one who repeats it. A *mantra* taken from a book, or from one who has not realized its full potential, is of little value; it is much like plugging an appliance into a wall outlet that has no electricity running to it.

The repetition of a *mantra* is called *japa*, and yogic practice of *mantra* repetition is called *japa* yoga.

Mantras:

Om Namah Shivaya (The great redeeming mantra): "Om, I honor the Supreme Self."

So'Ham (The sound of the ingoing and outgoing breath): "I am That."

Om Mani Padme Hum: (The oldest *mantra* of Tibetan Buddhism): "Om, jewel in the lotus, hum."

Namu Amida Butsu (From the Pure Land School of Buddhism): "I take refuge in the Amida Buddha."

"Lord Jesus Christ, have mercy on me" (The Jesus Prayer).

Maya (Sanskrit) ◆ The Sanskrit word for God's power of illusion, which brings about the whole world. This power causes the individual soul to believe that the unreal is real and that the transient is everlasting.

Maya is one of God's five powers, which are Creation, Sustenance, Dissolution, Concealment (*maya*) and Grace (Guru Principle).

Name ◆ God in the form of sound; the creative energy of God which creates this entire universe. Also called the Word; *Logos* (Greek) and *Shakti* (Sanskrit).

"In the beginning was the Word, and the Word was with God and the Word was God." (Saint John).

Om (Sanskrit) ◆ The primordial sound-vibration of the universe and the essence of all *mantras*.

Shakti (Sanskrit) ◆ The all-pervasive, creative energy of the Absolute Being; the power of Shiva. Also called *Chiti* (Sanskrit), *Sophia* (Greek), and *Te* (Chinese). The form of this supreme energy that illumines the human body and—when awakened by a Master—that removes every physical and spiritual block on the path to enlightenment, is called *kundalini*.

Shaktipat (Sanskrit) ◆ Literally, "the descent of Shakti." Specifically it refers to the transmission of spiritual energy from Master to disciple and the awakening of the *kundalini* energy that lies dormant at the base of the *sushumna* in the subtle body (corresponding to the spinal cord in the physical body). This awakening is the single most important step for one seeking liberation. *Shaktipat* can be given in four ways: by the Guru's touch, word, look, or will (*sankalpa*).

Shams-e Tabriz (Persia, 13th century) ◆ A wandering dervish from Tabriz, a city in northern Iran. Shams was master and guide to Jalaluddin Rumi.

Shiva (Sanskrit) ◆ The all-pervasive, Supreme Reality; the Absolute; God. Shiva is said to be the Eternal Witness of the Universe and is often paired with Shakti, who creates this eternal dance for Shiva's delight.

Shiva is also the name for one of the gods in the Hindu trinity, representing God's power of destruction.

Siddha (Sanskrit) ◆ From the Sanskrit, meaning "perfect." A perfect being; one who has attained Self-realization.

Siddha Yoga (Sanskrit) ◆ The yoga (path to union with God) based on one's relationship with a Siddha, a perfect Master, both outwardly, and inwardly. This is the "yoga of grace," which encompasses all the other forms of yoga and unfolds spontaneously in the disciple once his dormant spiritual energy has been awakened.

Although existing in unbroken lineage for thousands of years, it was shaped into a form of practices and teachings, and brought to the West by Swami Muktananda. When he died in 1982, the power of the lineage was passed on to his successor, Gurumayi Chidvilasananda.

Six Realms of Experience (Buddhism) ◆ The realms of experience that beings undergo in the endless cycle of birth and death; these are the realms of hell, unhappy ghosts, beasts, demons, humans, and celestial beings.

Sophia (Greek) ◆ The Supreme Creative Power of God; the source of all wisdom; *Chiti* (Sanskrit), *Shakti* (Sanskrit), *Te* (Chinese).

Sufi (Persian) ◆ One who belongs to the mystical sect of Islam based on love and devotion.

Tao (Chinese) ◆ A symbolic word from the Chinese that literally means "path," or "way," *Tao* is used to designate the one, impersonal, formless Absolute, from which the entire universe has evolved and to which it will return.

Te (Chinese) ◆ The universal power, *Tao*, embodied in a form or acting through a person; the qualities or virtues a thing receives from *Tao* making it what it is. A literal translation, derived from the Chinese pictograph, might read: "perfect action of mind and heart," or "a heart and mind which do not deviate from the truth." Most often, however, *Te* is translated as "virtue" in the classic sense of the Latin word *virtus*, meaning the "inherent quality or power latent in a thing." However, *Te* is not a moral concept but a clear reflection of the virtues of the universe, such as goodness, love, compassion, generosity, and humility.

"The result of a pure eye is sight; the result of a pure ear is hearing; the result of a pure mouth is taste; the result of a pure mind is wisdom; the result of pure wisdom is *Te*" (Chuang Tzu).

Vedas (Sanskrit) ◆ From the Sanskrit, meaning "knowledge," or "sacred teachings," the Vedas are the sacred scriptures which form the foundation of the Hindu religion. The four Vedas are the Rig Veda, the Veda of hymns; the Yajur Veda, the Veda of sacrificial texts; the Sama Veda, the Veda of songs; and the Atharva Veda, the Veda of Atharva, overseer of the sacred fire ceremony.

Vishnu (Sanskrit) ◆ The Supreme Lord who sustains the righteousness and truth of the universe.

We (Sufism) ◆ In Islamic and Sufi verse, God refers to Himself in the plural, as "We" or "Us," and not the singular.

Yoga (Sanskrit) ◆ From the Sanskrit *yug*, meaning "union," yoga is the practice that leads the individual soul to union with God. This union can be accomplished, with the guidance of a Master, through many different forms of yoga: *bhakti* yoga (union through devotion); *dhyana* yoga (union through meditation); *hatha* yoga (union through purification of the subtle body); *japa* yoga (union through the repetition of a sacred word); *karma* yoga (union through selfless service); *Siddha* yoga (union through the grace of a Master).

Zen (Japanese) ♦ A school of Buddhism that stresses the importance of enlightenment through the practice of *zazen*, sitting in a meditative, thought-free state. Essential to Zen practice is the special transmission from Master to disciple, insight into the nature of one's own mind, and direct experience of knowledge. (See **Dhyana Yoga**.)

Sources

THE SCRIPTURES OF INDIA

THE RIG VEDA
Rendered by Jonathan Star from Book X, 129.

Sources:

Koller, John M. *Oriental Philosophies.* New York: Scribner's Sons, 1985.

Prabhavananda, Swami. *The Spiritual Heritage of India.* Hollywood, CA: Vedanta Press, 1979.

Prabhavananda, Swami. *A Vedic Reader.* London: Oxford University Press, 1917.

THE UPANISHADS
All selections rendered by Jonathan Star.

Sources:

Hume, Robert E., trans. *The Thirteen Principal Upanishads.* London: Oxford University Press, 1921.

Prabhavananda, Swami, and Manchester, F., trans. *The Upanishads, Breath of the Eternal.* Hollywood, CA: Vedanta Press, 1948.

Sharma, D. S., trans. *The Upanishads, an Anthology.* Bombay: Bharatiya Vidya Bhavan, 1961.

Sri Purohit, Swami, and Yeats, W. B., trans. *The Ten Principal Upanishads.* London: Faber and Faber, 1937.

THE BHAGAVAD GITA
Selection on pp. 9–12 from Chapter 10, translated by Jonathan Star and Julle Lal.

Selection on pp. 13–17 from Chapter 11, translated by Jonathan Star and Julle Lal.

Selection on pp. 18–19 from Chapter 18, translated by Jonathan Star and Julle Lal.

Sources:

Anilbaran, Roy, ed. *The Gita.* Pondicherry: Sri Aurobindo Ashram, 1946.

Miller, Barbara Stoller, trans. *The Bhagavad-Gita.* New York: Bantam Doubleday Dell, 1986.

Prabhavananda, Swami, and Isherwood, Christopher, trans. *The Song of God: Bhagavad Gita.* Hollywood, CA.: Vedanta Press, 1944.

Radhakrishnan, S., trans. *The Bhagavad Gita*. New York: Harper & Row, 1948.
Sargeant, Winthrop, trans. *The Bhagavad Gita*. Albany, NY: SUNY Press, 1984.
Tapasyananda, Swami, trans. *Srimad Bhagavadgita*. Mylapore, Madras: Sri Ramakrishna Math.

THE AVADHUTA GITA
All selections rendered by Jonathan Star.

Sources:
Ashokananda, Swami, trans. *Avadhuta Gita of Dattatreya*. Mylapore, Madras: Sri Ramakrishna Math, 1981.
Chetanananda, Swamin. *Avadhuta Gita: Song of the Ever-Free*. Calcutta: Advaita Ahrama, 1984.
Sri Purohit, Swami. *Avadhoota Gita*. New Delhi: Munishiram Manoharlal, 1979.

THE VISHNU SAHASRANAM
Rendered by Jonathan Star.

Sources:
Barrack, Howard J., trans. *The Thousand Names of Vishnu*. New York: Tara Publications, 1974.
The Nectar of Chanting. South Fallsburg, NY: SYDA Foundation, 1975.
Tapasyananda, Swami, trans. *Sri Vishnu Sahasranam*. Mylapore, Madras: Sri Ramakrishna Math, 1986.

THE SAGES OF TAOISM

TAO TE CHING
All selections from: Star, Jonathan, trans. Tao Te Ching. Princeton, NJ: Theone Press, 1988.

CHUANG TZU
All selections rendered by Jonathan Star. Selections from Chapters 2, 4, 14, and 19 of Chuang Tzu.

Sources:
Giles, Lionel, trans. *Chuang Tzu*. London: Unwin Paperbacks, 1980.
Watson, Burton, trans. *The Complete Works of Chuang Tzu*. New York: Columbia University Press, 1968.

Yutang, Lin, trans. *The Wisdom of Lao Tzu.* New York: The Modern Library, 1948.

LIEH TZU

Translated by Tzu-jan Wu.

THE BUDDHIST MASTERS

SHAKYAMUNI BUDDHA
All selections from: Lal, P., trans. The Dhammapada. *New York: Farrrar, Straus and Giroux, 1967, pp. 11, 18–20, 31.*

THE DHAMMAPADA
All selections rendered by Jonathan Star.

Sources:
Babbitt, Irving, trans. *The Dhammapada.* New York: Oxford University Press, 1936.

Easwaran, Ednath, trans. *The Dhammapada.* Petaluma, CA: Nilgiri Press, 1985.

Lal, P., trans., *The Dhammapada.* New York: Farrrar, Straus, and Giroux, 1967.

Maitreya, B. Ananda, trans. *The Dhammapada, the Path of Truth.* Novato, CA: Lotsawa, 1988.

Muller, Max, trans. *The Dhammapada.* Sacred Books of the East. New York: Collier and Son, 1900.

EIHEI DOGEN
All selections from: Tanahashi, Kazuaki, ed. Moon in a Dewdrop: Writings of Zen Master Dogen. *San Francisco: North Point Press, 1985, pp. 34–35.*

BASSUI ZENJI
All selections from: Kapleau, Philip. The Three Pillars of Zen. *Boston: Beacon Press, 1965, pp. 160–161, 164, 169.*

HUANG PO
All selections from: Blofeld, John, trans. The Zen Teachings of Huang Po. *New York: Grove Press, 1958, pp. 29–30, 35–36, 131.*

YOKA DAISHI
All selections from: Suzuki, D. T. Manual of Zen Buddhism. *New York: Grove Press, 1960, pp. 97–100.*

SHANTIDEVA
All selections from: Burtt, E. A., trans. Teachings of the Compassionate Buddha. *New York: New American Library, 1955, pp. 135, 137.*

GIZAN
Selected from: Stryk, W., and Ikemoto, T. Zen Poems of China. Garden City, NY: Anchor Press, 1973, p. 69.

WISDOM OF THE HEBREWS

THE BOOK OF PSALMS
All selections rendered by Jonathan Star.

THE WISDOM OF SOLOMON
All selections rendered by Jonathan Star.
Selection on p. 75 from Chapter 6.
Selection on pp. 76–78 from Chapter 7.
Selection on p. 79 from Chapters 8 and 9.

ECCLESIASTICUS (SIRACH)
All sections adapted from The New English Bible. *New York: Oxford University Press, 1961.*
Selection on pp. 80–81 from Chapter 24, verses 1–6, 9–22
Selection on p. 82 from Chapter 1, verses 1–10, and Chapter 4, verses 11–13.
Selection on p. 83 from Chapter 6, verses 23–30, 36

Sources:
The New English Bible. New York: Oxford University Press, 1961.
New American Standard Bible. Carol Stream, IL: Creation House, Inc., 1960.

THE STOIC PHILOSOPHERS

MARCUS AURELIUS
All selections rendered by Jonathan Star.
Selection on p. 87 from Book 5:1 and Book 7:69.

Selection on p. 88 from Book 2:4 and Book 2:17.
Selection on p. 89 from Book 7:13, Book 11:9, and Book 6:44.
Selection on p. 90 from Book 8:50 and Book 5:6.
Selection on p. 91 from Book 7:68.
Selection on p. 92 from Book 10:38, Book 5:21, and Book 7:59.
Selection on p. 93 from Book 8:34, Book 4:23, and Book 10:16

Sources:
Haines, C. R., trans. *Marcus Aurelius.* Cambridge, MA: Harvard University Press, 1916.
Long, George, trans. *The Meditations of Marcus Aurelius.* New York: The Harvard Classics, P. F. Collier and Son, 1909.
Rendall, G. H., trans. *Marcus Aurelius Antoninus to Himself.* London: Macmillan and Co., 1898.
Staniforth, Maxwell, trans. *Marcus Aurelius: Meditations.* New York: Penguin Books, 1964.

EPICTETUS
All selections adapted from: Crossley, Hastings, trans. The Golden Sayings of Epictetus. *New York: P. F. Collier and Son, 1909, verses 1, 66, 77.*

SENECA
All selections adapted from: Davis, Chas. Greek and Roman Stoicism. *Boston: Herbert B. Turner and Co., 1903, pp. 226, 236, 241.*

THE SUFI POETS

JALALUDDIN RUMI
All selections from: Star, Jonathan, and Shiva, Shahram, trans. A Garden Beyond Paradise. *New York: Bantam Books, 1992, except selections on pp. 114–117, entitled "Your Triumphant Song" and "A Sacred Blasphemy," from: Star, Jonathan, trans.* Rumi: In the Arms of the Beloved. *New York: Tarcher/Putnam, 1997.*

HAFEZ
All selections rendered by Jonathan Star

Sources:
Avery, Peter, and Heath-Stubbs, John, trans. *Hafiz of Shiraz.* London: John Murray, 1952.
Boylan, Michael. *Hafez: Dance of Life.* Washington, DC: Mage Publications, 1987.

Clark, H. Wilberforce, trans. *The Divan-i Hafiz*, Vols. 1 and 2. London: The Octagon Press, 1974.

Hillman, Michael. *Unity in the Ghazals of Hafez*. Chicago: Bibliotheca Islamica, 1976.

Persia Society of London. *Selections from the Rubaiyat and Odes of Hafiz*. London: John M. Watkins, 1920.

IBN AL ARABI

Adapted by Jonathan Star from: Manheim, Ralph, trans. Creative Imagination in the Sufism of Ibn 'Arabi. *Princeton, NJ: Princeton University Press, 1969, pp. 174–175.*

FAKHRUDDIN ARAQI

All selections translated by Shahram Shiva and Jonathan Star from: La' amat (Divine Flashes), *flashes 7, 14, 25, 27.*

Source:

Chittick, William C., and Wilson, Peter L., trans. *Fakhruddin 'Iraqi: Divine Flashes*. New York: Paulist Press, 1982.

JAMI

Adapted by Jonathan Star from: Nicholson, R. H. The Mystics of Islam. *New York: Shocken Books, 1975, p. 81.*

MAHMUD SHABISTARI

All selections rendered by Jonathan Star.

Sources:

Lederer, Florence, trans. *The Secret Rose Garden*. Grand Rapids, MI: Phanes Press, 1987.

Whinfield, E. H., trans. *The Secret Rose Garden*. London, 1880.

GHALIB

All selections translated by Jonathan Star.

Source:

Ahmad, Aijaz, trans. *The Ghazals of Ghalib*. New York: Columbia University Press, 1971, ghazals 1, 4.

NAZIR

Adapted by Jonathan Star from: Behari, Bankey. Sufis, Mystics and Yogis of India. *Bombay: Bharatiya Vidya Bhavan, 1982, pp. 183–188.*

BABA KUHI OF SHIRAZ
Selection from: Nicholson, Reynold, trans. Translations of Eastern Poetry *and Prose. New York: Greenwood Press, 1969, p. 101.*

THE CHRISTIAN SAINTS

SAINT PAUL
Selection on "Love," pp. 151–152, rendered by Jonathan Star from I Corinthians 13:1–13.
All other selections from The New English Bible. *New York: Oxford University Press, 1961.*
"The Apostles," p. 153, from I Corinthians 4:8–13 and II Corinthians 6:4–10.
"The Spirit," p. 154, from I Corinthians 12:4–11 and I Corinthians 3:16–17.

THE PHILOKALIA
All selections from: Kadloubovsky, E., and Palmer, G. E. H., trans. Early Fathers from the Philokalia. *London: Faber and Faber Limited, 1954, pp. 109, 157–158, 161, 166, 170.*

MEISTER ECKHART
All selections adapted by Jonathan Star from: Pfeiffer, Franz, and Evans, C. de B., trans. Meister Eckhart. *London: John M. Watkins, 1924, 1931, Vol. 1: 118, 157, 221–222, 287, 338, 348, 363, 429, and Vol. 2: 41, 114.*
Source:
Blakney, Raymond B., trans. *Meister Eckhart.* New York: Harper and Row, 1941.

RUSSIAN MONK
All selections from: French, R. M., trans. The Way of a Pilgrim. *New York: The Seabury Press, 1965, pp. 1, 7, 31, 41, 105.*

THOMAS À KEMPIS
All selections from: Whitford, Richard, trans. The Imitation of Christ, *adapted by Harold C. Gardiner. New York: Doubleday and Co., 1955, pp. 109–111.*

JEAN PIERRE DE CAUSSADE

All selections from: Beevers, John, trans. Abandonment to Divine Providence. *New York: Doubleday, 1975, pp. 25, 37, 40, 70, 73, 81–82, except "The Sacredness of Every Moment," p. 168, and "There is nothing faith . . .," p. 171 from: Ramiere, Rev. H., trans.* Abandonment. *New York: Benziger Brothers, 1887, pp. 79, 112, and "O Lord, let others . . ," p. 170, rendered by Jonathan Star.*

THE POET-SAINTS OF INDIA

SHANKARACHARYA

Selections on pp. 178 and 180–181 rendered by Jonathan Star. Selection on p. 179 is from: Prabhavananda, Swami, and Isherwood, Christopher, trans. Shankara's Crest-Jewel of Discrimination. *New York: New American Library, 1947, pp. 119–127.*

KABIR

All selections rendered by Jonathan Star, from literal translations supplied by Krishan Bakshi, Vinod Argawal, and Anand Mundra.

Source:
Tagore, Rabindranath, trans. *Songs of Kabir.* York Beach, ME: Samuel Weiser, 1977.

TUKARAM

Selection on p. 186 was adapted by Jonathan Star from: Hoyland, John S., trans. An India Peasant Mystic. *Dublin, IN: Prinit Press, 1932, pp. 43, 47. All other selections are from: Ranade, R. D.* Mysticism in India. *Albany, NY: SUNY Press, 1983, pp. 303, 312, 320, 339, 349.*

MIRABAI

All selections rendered by Jonathan Star.

Sources:
Dingra, Baldoon, trans. *Songs of Meera.* New Delhi: Vision Books, 1977.
Poddar, Hanumanprasad. *The Philosophy of Love. Bhakti Sutras of Devarsi Narada.* Orissa, India: Orissa Cement Ltd., 1980.

AKKAMAHADEVI

All selections adapted from: Ramanujan, A. K., trans. Speaking of Shiva. *New York: Penguin Books, 1973, pp. 118, 122, 139.*

RAMDASA

All selections from Ranade, R. D. Mysticism in India. *Albany, NY: SUNY Press, 1983, pp. 390–392, 395, 410, 412–413, 415.*

JNANESHWAR

Translated by Jonathan Star and Julle Lal from the Amritanubhava, *Chapter 1, except the selections on p. 211, which are from: Bahirat, B. P., trans.* The Philosophy of Jnanadeva. *Bombay: Popular Book Depot, 1956, pp. 150, 151, and the selection on p. 212, which is from Kripananda, Swami.* Jnaneshwar's Gita. *Albany, NY: SUNY Press, 1989, p. 350.*

SWAMI MUKTANANDA

Selection on "The Guru," p. 213, is from: Muktananda, Swami. I Have Become Alive. *South Fallsburg, NY: SYDA Foundation, 1985, p. 29, and from a lecture given in Miami, Florida, 1980.*

Selections on "Perfect Beings," p. 214, are from a talk given in Ganeshpuri, India, 1983, and Darshan Magazine, Vol. 30/31:162 (1989).

Selection on "The World," p. 215, is from: Muktananda, Swami. I Have Become Alive. *South Fallsburg, NY: SYDA Foundation, 1985, pp. 147, 172, 203.*

Selection on "Love," pp. 216–217, is from: Muktananda, Swami. I Have Become Alive. *South Fallsburg, NY: SYDA Foundation, 1985, pp. 175–177, 183.*

Selection on "The Universal Energy," p. 218, is from: Muktananda, Swami. Siddha Meditation. *South Fallsburg, NY: SYDA Foundation, 1977, p. 60.*

Selection on "The Final Realization," p. 219, is from: Muktananda, Swami. Play of Consciousness. *South Fallsburg, NY: SYDA Foundation, 1978, p. 183.*

Selection on "The Kingdom Within," pp. 220–222, is from an unpublished work written in 1972.

Grateful acknowledgment is made for permission to reprint the following:
Excerpts from *Tao Te Ching*, trans. by Jonathan Star, reprinted by permission of Theone Press. Copyright © 1988 by Jonathan Star.
Excerpts from *Manual of Zen Buddhism*, by D. T. Suzuki, reprinted by permission of The Random Century Group Ltd. and Grove Weidenfeld, a division of Grove Press, Inc.
Excerpts from *The Zen Teachings of Huang Po*, by John Blofeld, reprinted by permission of Grove Weidenfeld, a division of Grove Press, Inc. Copyright © 1958 by John Blofeld.
Excerpts from *Teachings of the Compassionate Buddha*, trans. by E. A. Burtt, reprinted by permission of Penguin USA.
Excerpts from *The Path of Light*, by J. D. Barnett, reprinted by permission of John Murray Publishers Ltd.
Excerpts from *Moon in a Dewdrop: Writings of Zen Master Dogen*, edited by Kazuaki Tanahashi, reprinted by permission of North Point Press. Copyright © 1985 by The San Francisco Zen Center.
Excerpts from *The Three Pillars of Zen*, by Philip Kapleau, reprinted by permission of Doubleday, a division of Bantam Doubleday Dell Publishing Group, and Century Hutchinson Publishing. Copyright © 1965, 1989 by Phillip Kapleau. Copyright © 1980 by The Zen Center, Inc.
Excerpts from *Zen Poems of China*, by Lucien Stryk, Takashi Ikemoto, and Taigan Takayama, reprinted by permission of Doubleday, a division of Bantam Doubleday Dell Publishing Group. Copyright © 1973 by Lucien Stryk, Takashi Ikemoto, and Taigan Takayama.
Excerpts from *Creative Imagination in the Sufism of Ibn 'Arabi*, trans. by Ralph Manheim, reprinted by permission of Princeton University Press.
Excerpt from *Translations of Eastern Poetry and Prose*, trans. by Reynold Nicholson, reprinted by permission of Greenwood Press.
Excerpts from *New English Bible*, reprinted by permission of Oxford University Press.
Excerpts from *Early Fathers from the Philokalia*, trans. by E. Kadloubovsky and G. E. H. Palmer, reprinted by permission of Faber and Faber Ltd.
Excerpts from *The Way of a Pilgrim*, trans. by R. M. French, reprinted by permission of HarperCollins Publishers. Copyright © 1965 by Eleanor French.
Excerpts from *The Imitation of Christ by Thomas à Kempis*, trans. by Harold C. Gardiner, trans. copyright © 1955. Used by permission of Doubleday, a division of Bantam Doubleday Dell Publishing Group, Inc.

About the Author

Jonathan Star graduated with honors from Harvard University, where he studied Eastern religion and architecture. For the past fifteen years he has pursued spiritual practice, both Zen Meditation and Yogic disciplines.

Mr. Star's poetry and writings have been translated into several languages. His works include *Rumi: In the Arms of the Beloved, A Garden Beyond Paradise,* and a translation of the *Tao Te Ching.*